# TEN COUNT
## — THE BOOK —
### ESTD 2016

**DAVE MILAM & CHAD SIMPKINS**
PLUS 15 ADDITIONAL CONTRIBUTORS

ISBN-978-1530740093
ISBN-10: 1530740096

# TEN COUNT

## THE BOOK

### ESTD 2016

# CONTENTS

# ROUND TWO: ON THE ROPES

# ROUND THREE: STANDING EIGHT COUNT

# ROUND FOUR: THROWING IN THE TOWEL

# CONTRIBUTORS

# ACKNOWLEDGEMENTS

What you are about to read is the culmination of years of struggle and countless sleepless nights from leaders across the country. The toil and triumph represented in these pages pales in comparison to the overwhelming faithfulness of God found in the midst of pain. Few leaders were willing to vulnerably reveal their darkest moments and allow their heartache to become part of your healing.

This book would not be possible without the contributors who were willing to be open, honest, raw and vulnerable: expressions many pastors are afraid to show. Thank you to each writer for their time, effort, and for sharing their Ten Count moments.

From Dave Milam: Thanks to Chad Simpkins who was the catalyst and administrative wizard behind this project. Your steadiness and character is impeccable and I'm grateful to be your friend.

To my wife, Anne, who saw something special in a shaggy headed young man so many years ago; your steady encouragement, combined with your skill and precision as an editor, has made this book possible. Thank you for taking care of the kids without complaint, and for making sure there's an ample supply of frozen pizzas available when I'm too busy to make dinner. I am grateful for your faithfulness during the hard times that forged a depth in our marriage that plunged us beyond the shallow years of our youth. The story that our lives are writing is my most cherished possession.

From Chad Simpkins: A big thanks to my wife Kara. The stories I share in this book are her stories too. Our shared experiences made us stronger together. Thanks for being my partner in ministry and in life! I look forward to seeing the stories we continue to write.

And thanks to Dave Milam. This book doesn't exist without you starting a conversation with me a little over a year ago. Funny how we both felt the urge to share stories to help others in ministry. Now here we are. Your heart for planters and pastors is contagious and because of that, this book will begin to heal others. Thanks for making this happen!

# TEN COUNT
# INTRODUCTION
★★★★★

# INTRODUCTION

Hunched over a plate of scrambled eggs, he sat gripping his coffee as if the ceramic mug were his lifeline. Face turned downward, he spoke with a forlorn tone. This was not the breakfast appointment I had expected. Something was sadly different.

He used to be fearless, passionate and full of faith. Like a headline fighter explodes into the arena through a wall of applause and smoke, he once walked bold and strong. After dozens of body blows and several bloody rounds, he now sat bruised, cut and waiting for the fight to be over.

Outmatched and on the ropes, my battle worn breakfast companion had heard the "Ten Count." His hunger to fight was gone. The ring had changed him forever.

Like my friend, tales of struggle, loneliness, and failure have become commonplace among Christian entrepreneurs, pastors, and church planters around the world. For many of us, exhaustion replaces the adrenaline that once surged when we stepped into the ring. Now we stand with weak knees, sucking wind upon a blood splattered canvas.

Exhausted and cynical, we have experienced the ten count.

This book is an honest collection of stories from Christian leaders who, admittedly, have been clocked by life, and have experienced the Ten Count. These are the stories of leaders who entered the ring against an opponent which had outranked, outsized, and out-matched them and found themselves face down on the mat.

I'll warn you, these stories are extremely raw and some readers may be offended by them, but they're real. You are likely to never hear these stories on the main stage of a conference or published in the glossy pages of a Christian magazine. But these stories need to be told. If you are looking for feel good, pastors-are-saints stories, put this book down now, and walk away. These stories come from a vulnerable place, deep within the soul of each writer. They may even articulate your story, in the ring where you are fighting.

Our desire for this book is to begin a sacred conversation that helps those who are experiencing a Ten Count and to give others a peek into the lives of leaders fighting the hardest brawl of their lives. Our hope is it will apply a little salve to the cuts above your eyes, some ice to your sore muscles and maybe a few stitches if needed.

These are our Ten Count stories.

# OUTMATCHED
### AND OVERPOWERED

ROUND ONE

## - OUTMATCHED -

# ENOUGH

*by Dave Milam*

Our first church office rested on the second floor in a small business park above a doctor's office. White walls and three cubicles were precisely spread throughout the small room to nest the activity for the first few years of our church's life. It was an eclectic mishmash of chairs and office furniture, most left behind by the previous tenants.

Monday mornings buzzed with activity. Volunteers banged out the previous day's follow-up with the tiktak sounds of typing and I analyzed our weekly attendance stats. I'm a visual thinker so I enjoyed plotting our growth on paper.

My graph was a tattered sheet of paper I had hidden in the back of a recycled three ring binder. By design, my tallies landed near the bottom of the page offering acres of room above for upward growth. Like a small child scoring his height on a bedroom wall, week by week I scribbled down our totals and would daydream of a trend-line that would thrust us into the stratosphere.

Occasionally the chart dipped. Mother's day was the worst. Even the crickets went somewhere else to visit family on that day. Each number wielded a strange voodoo kinda power over me. When the attendance dipped, so did my morale. When it exceeded the previous week, I smiled. Mondays were like Groundhog Day for my staff—watching my head pop out of the cubicle would forecast the week's temperature.

Over time, attendance flat-lined. The lines on my tattered graph began resembling a dead man's cardiac monitor. I was fearful we were doomed. Something needed to jolt our church back into an upward trend. Stagnation was not an option.

I stared at the books on my shelf wondering which one would provide the right amount of fiction to get us moving again. I wasn't prepared for a recession this early. We were only one year old.

I was confident that our sluggish growth was a leadership issue; my issue. Only two months earlier, I sat elbow to elbow in a crowded arena listening to leadership guru, John Maxwell. He blubber that "Everything rises and falls on leadership" from the main stage. I believed it was my sole responsibly to restart our growth engine.

Maybe we weren't working hard enough.

I slid out one of Maxwell's many leadership books and thumbed through the pages hoping that a quick fix would leap from the hardback. John offered no solutions. I took a long deep breathe and concluded, "I guess we're just gonna have to work even harder."

In the center of our office space was a small meeting room with a large black table fashioned from old barn wood. Reclaimed wood wasn't the rage then, but cheap was. To the left of the table sat a wall painted to double as a chalkboard for brainstorming. It was there I would craft our plan.

I stood chalking the wall like a crazed Russell Crowe in a Beautiful Mind, madly flowcharting strategies and systems for the next season. Our solution: more marketing, more groups and better doughnuts.

I stepped back from the wall to admire the new lineup and prayed, "God, our family's schedule will be unmanageable for the next season, but if that's what it's gonna take, Lord, we'll do it."

Postcards were sent and full page ads glossed the back cover of local magazines. We even upgraded the doughnuts in the lobby. Between breakfast bible studies and evening life groups, my wife and I were leading five small communities and training leaders as efficiently as possible. I knew the pace wasn't sustainable. But somehow, we had to fast track discipleship. We desperately needed leaders.

My Monday morning graphing routine quickly vanished under the pressure of a new schedule. My desk testified to my state of mind; suffocated with stacks of paper, books and unopened mail. Near the bottom of the pile hid my worn out recycled three ring binder.

Months of ignoring our numbers birthed a curiosity in me. I wondered if our efforts made any statistical impact. So, with pen in hand, I swiped clean an area of my desk and sat down. Meticulously, I plotted each week's attendance and leaned back with a sigh. Our trend line had bumped up by one tick-mark then returned to her lifeless state.

Nothing had changed.

Taco salad and a planning meeting were on the menu for lunch. I knew I was supposed to eat. After all, I had paid a fortune for a plate of meat and greens. But all I could do was push the food around with my fork. My stomach was in knots and just couldn't handle one bite.

I was quiet most of the meal, then broke my silence, "Does anybody have any idea what's going to get our church growing again?"

Nobody answered. We were all overextended and couldn't see clearly.

One of my leaders had been reading Jim Cymbala's book, Fresh Wind Fresh Fire and was young, confident and hard headed. Without skipping a beat, he looked me straight in the eye and said, "It's easy. The problem is that we are not spiritual enough. The Brooklyn Tabernacle started really growing when they began a prayer meeting. If we would just pray and fast more, God would bless us."

What he said made some sense. Perhaps God was just waiting for us to step back and look for Him to do the work. Maybe we were trying too hard and needed to turn our faces toward God as the solution.

We didn't have any other answers, so we officially instituted a weekly prayer time before each service. Every volunteer, after unloading all of our gear and setting up our church, was expected to join our church's weekly prayer time before serving. We were really going for it. Expectations were high and Jim Cymbala would have been proud.

We prayed hard and the chart did not respond.

Weeks into our spiritual "revival," the phone rang. On the other end I heard the voice of a young church planter named Steven. Steven had big plans to launch a new church in Charlotte. He and his team were doing research and wanted to see how we navigated a movie theater on Sunday mornings. Calls like this were routine, so I welcomed them knowing his team might bump our numbers for one week. Win-win.

That Sunday, we had a few extra hands and a small attendance bump. Steven was skinny, sincere and wore a buzzed haircut. He offered to buy lunch for a mid-week follow up meeting and I felt I hit the jackpot.

Logan's Roadhouse was one of my favorite lunch stops of the day. The unpolished blue collar feel of peanuts on the ground made me feel at home. Steven and I talked shop and he took notes for most of our meal. His team was still in the planning stages of their plant. As our lunch concluded, Steven slid his checkbook from his back pocket and scribbled out a check to help support our church from his personal account. I deposited it immediately and we began a rhythm of meeting. This guy was the real deal and I enjoyed his perspective on life and leadership.

Several months passed before we landed back at Logan's. This time, we sat at a different booth but in the same section. Our waitress was well seasoned and on time with the Diet Coke refills. I order a Grilled Chicken sandwich and Steven ordered a cranberry juice. The order was quite a diversion from his normal burger and fries.

Curious, I asked, "Dude, did you already eat lunch today?"

He smiled and sipped his juice, chuckled and said, "No."

The waitress slid a basket of hot rolls onto the table. Steven looked away and I knew what was going on. "You're fasting aren't you?" I said.

"Well…yes," he said sheepishly.

"Sweet. Pass me the peanuts." I taunted then continued, "So are you planning to eat after the sun goes down or are you going to pound a huge breakfast in the morning?"

He passed the galvanized peanut bucket and answered. "I guess you could say that I'm on an extended fast."

It was a Zero Dark Thirty moment and he was being evasive. I amped up the intensity and insisted, "Seriously. How long are your fasting, three days…a week, what?"

There was a long thoughtful pause before he answered. "Well, I'm two days into my first forty day fast. Our church is launching soon, so I wanted to fast and pray as we get started. You could join me if you wanted."

A forty day fast had been on my bucket list for years. A spiritual discipline at that level would surely get God's attention. After all, our prayer service had done nothing. Maybe this would move God to bless us.

"I'll need to check with my wife before I commit, but I'd really like to join you," I replied.


I'm not sure my wife knew what she was agreeing to. Forty days is a long time and low blood sugar can make a man pretty grumpy. I jumped in with Steven. We were two dedicated church planters storming the throne-room of heaven on behalf of our churches.

Steven broke his forty day with Mexican and warned me of the consequences of too much too quickly. So, I was much more cautious and eased out gently. He launched his church and I continued leading mine.

Over the next two years, we met less frequently. His church exploded and mine maintained. I pushed through three more forty day fasts and couldn't figure out what I needed to do to get God's attention. Why wouldn't He bless us? I was leading well, working hard and praying fervently—but our attendance remained virtually flat.

Steven and I met a handful of times after our forty day fast, so I mostly lost track of him. One day, I got curious about their epic growth and popped open my computer. Bad decision.

A few clicks into my Google search, I bumped into a video that hypnotized me. My friend Steven sat calmly next to a local news anchor fielding questions about the tremendous growth of his church. I was intrigued, so I decided to watch.

The anchor asked, "Pastor Steven, we have seen your church grow from a small living room of people to a massive church in the thousands in just a couple of years. I'm curious, what do you think caused your church's unprecedented growth? How did that happen?"

The camera cut to a shot of Steven. He didn't hesitate, "That's a great question. And here's the answer: God blessed our church because we sacrificed and we fasted and we prayed. It's that simple. God honored us seeking Him. That's why our church was able to grow so quickly."

I stared at the screen and felt the blood rush out of my head. My ears and cheeks began to tingle. Then a tear formed in the corner of my eyes as the video's sound faded away.

Silence.

I whispered, "But I prayed and fasted too."

Silence.

It only took a few seconds to redefine success and to begin feeling like a complete failure as a church leader. They are big, we are small. God likes them, not us. They are winning, we are not.

The only way for me to make sense of their growth was to devalue it. I began thinking, "Well, they don't do small groups like we do" - or this famous line - "They just stole a bunch of members from other churches."

At that moment, it simply wasn't enough to devalue. I began hoping for God to stop using them; for their decline.

My heart was in a bad place and it really scared me.

That night, I laid in bed, stared at the ceiling and confided in my wife. It only took a few moments for her to care more about my spirit than my dreams. She became the woman I needed. She said, "Dave, you sound incredibly envious."

It was at that moment, I knew what it was like to be Cain when God blessed Abel's offering or Saul who was jealous of David's popularity among the people. I understood what it was like to have envy drive you to the point of hoping for the death of something God created and ordained.

I was wrong and needed to repent. I prayed for God to forgive me.

It's interesting that the second recorded sin in all of creation was this one. Ultimately, it is the result of the brokenness of mankind and the current condition of the heart of men. It keeps us from rejoicing when others rejoice and weeping when they weep. Scripture promises, envy will rot you from the inside out.

> A HEART AT PEACE GIVES LIFE TO THE BODY,
> BUT ENVY ROTS THE BONES.
> - PROVERBS 14:30 -

It's the pain of infertility and the jealousy of losing a promotion or contract. It's the resentment of being single when everyone's getting married.

It was at this moment I began to understand what it means to run the race set before me. It was not my job to run anybody else's race. God, in His infinite wisdom, had somehow determined I was the man for the job in my context. And in His grand masterplan, my only calling was to faithfully steward every opportunity the Lord set before me—to the best of my ability.

No more, no less.

A tattered graph in the back of a recycled three ring binder does not document my worth. I did not need to perform outrageous spiritual gymnastics or sacrifice my mental and emotional health to get God's attention. I already had His attention. The moment I accepted Christ was the moment I became enough. And the size of my church or the span of my influence would not make me more valuable to God.

I am enough.

## - OUTMATCHED -

# WHEN LIFE MEETS FAITH

*by Chad Simpkins*

It was early September and my wife Kara and I were getting ready for our small group to meet for the first time that fall. I was an Associate Pastor at a church in Princeton, NJ, and this was our first small group gathering as a couple. We lived on the second floor of a framing shop, on a tree lined street, on Main Street, in Pennington, NJ. A quaint town filled with old homes from years past. Our apartment was the top floor of that framing shop, built in 1798.

Thirty minutes before our group was scheduled to arrive, Kara shot past me heading to the door. She told me she needed to run to the store, she forgot something. I thought that was a bit strange with people showing up soon, but didn't think much about it. Fifteen minutes later, she walked in the front door, walked right past me, and went into the bathroom. Strange, but I figured she needed to go real bad.

A couple minutes later, Kara calls me into the bathroom. I figured she was sick and we were going to have to call off our group. I walked into the bathroom and she handed me this strange looking stick. "What is this?" I asked. She replied, "It's a pregnancy test. I'm pregnant." I looked at the stick, looked at her, looked at the stick again, then handed it to her and told her these sweet words, "We'll talk about this later. Our group is coming and we need to get ready."

Don't worry, I asked for forgiveness later.

We were pregnant. Our first child. Life was getting ready to change. Truthfully, in ways we could never imagine.

Four months into the pregnancy, Kara went in for one of her monthly check ups. There was no need for me to be there. It was all routine. At this appointment, Kara would give blood for an AFP test. This test was a routine screening for possible birth defects in your unborn child. When Kara finished her appointment that day, the nurse looked at her and told her, "If there are any problems, we'll call you back. But you should be fine. You're young and healthy."

The church I worked for was growing. So much so, we got rid of our separate offices to make room for more classroom space for our children's ministry. Inside the front doors stood our 'cafe.' All of the staff worked in that space. I was sitting at my cafe table working on upcoming events for the student ministry. A call came in to the office. Our secretary told me I had a call from my wife. This was a little unusual. Maybe she wants to go grab lunch? Maybe she made plans for the evening? Maybe she had to work later?

On the other end of the line, my wife is crying. Sobbing. Weeping. "What's wrong?! Are you ok?!"

Her words come back to me haunt me to this day. "I need you to come home now." I grabbed my stuff, ran out the door, and headed to our apartment. Once inside, I ran to our living room. There, sitting on our couch, tears streaming down her face, was my wife. "What is going on?" I asked. Kara proceeded to tell me that the nurse from her OBGYN office had called. Our AFP test came back positive for Down's Syndrome. They needed us in as soon as possible to see what was happening in the womb. I remember holding my wife tightly that day.

Kara's doctors sent us to the University of Pennsylvania Women's Hospital in Philadelphia for a Level 2 Diagnostic Ultrasound. After taking all the detailed pictures, measurements, and video they needed, they sent us back to the waiting room. We waited for what seemed like an eternity. Finally, they called us back to the doctor's office. We walked in. Behind an impressive mahogany desk stood a wall of video monitors. All videos and pictures of our child. It was amazing to see! Her movements, her twitches, her face, her body. She looked fine.

Then the news arrived.

A team of maternal fetal medicine specialists began to describe to us the state of our child. She had swelling around her neck. Her hands we abnormal and both feet were clubbed. Her heart had formed improperly. In fact, some of the chambers were missing. Her lymphatic system was nonexistent. She had fluid collecting around her brain. To us, her adoring parents, we saw this beautiful child on the monitors. She looked alive and active in the videos. Then the doctors uttered these words to us, "We have no idea how she is still alive."

I loved it! A fighting spirit! A strong child!

But the mood changed from bad to worse. The doctor's diagnosis was Down's Syndrome. Our daughter was a severe case, which involved insurmountable heart defects. "She should be dead." They kept saying that sentence over and over again. Finally the doctors told us, "She is going to die at some point before birth, we strongly recommend termination of the pregnancy immediately, for your (Kara's) safety."

Your child is going to die soon. Your wife's life MIGHT be at stake if you continue the pregnancy. What do you do? Kara and I looked at each other. We looked back at the team of doctors. Without hesitation we told them that termination was not an option for us. The doctors were accepting of our response. They reiterated the outcome for our daughter and possible outcome for Kara. We understood what they were saying. They told us there was nothing they could do, but that Kara would need to go in every week to monitor the situation.

We left the hospital that day torn apart. How could this happen to us? We were young. My wife was very healthy - she was a personal trainer, studied it in college - she knew how to take care of herself. WE WERE CHRISTIANS! IN MINISTRY! God, really?

We didn't throw in the towel though. We were not resigned to the doctor's prognosis. We began to express some positive vibes for this moment in our lives together. We knew God was going to do a miracle. We knew God was going to redeem this situation. We knew God was going to heal our child so the doctors could understand God had more power and knowledge than them. People were praying. We were praying. We lived by faith!

It was a cold morning on January 27th, 2001. My wife, her mom and I piled into our car and drove down to the UPenn Women's Hospital again. This time it wasn't for an ultrasound, or a check up, or anything hopeful. This time it was for Kara to give birth to our daughter - Kendall Grace Simpkins - seven months into her pregnancy. Not a live birth mind you. A stillbirth. Earlier that week, we went in for our check up. No heartbeat. Kendall had passed away. An induction was unavoidable.

Imagine giving birth to a child you will never hold, never feed, never play with, never teach to ride a bike, never laugh with, never spend time with. That day was terrible in so many ways. The doctors began the process of labor early that morning hoping to get us in and out as fast as possible. Due to a terrible accident in Philadelphia earlier that day, Kara's doctors couldn't get her back to the OR when they wanted. We waited. Twelve long hours later, Kendall was stillborn. Can you imagine watching your wife be in labor all day long, KNOWING no child was going home with you? I wanted to take her place so badly that day.

To make matters worse, we were in the Labor and Delivery ward. You would think they would have a special, quiet corner of the hospital set aside for situations like ours. Not the case. As they wheeled Kara out of her room and down the hall towards the OR, we were bombarded with new parents videoing their newborn babies. I vividly remember watching a set of grandparents smile with joy as they welcomed new life into their family. All I saw were smiles and happiness and joy and I just wanted to scream from the top of my lungs, "Shut the ___ up!" Their happiness was suffocating. Finally, around 10 p.m. we were done. Kara, her mom, and I solemnly got back into our car and drove home. Empty armed. Torn. Bitter. Beat up. Tired. Done.

I was mad. No, angry is a better word. Not at anyone. At God. Furious at God. I could not figure out how this happened. We were young and healthy and Christians and working in a church. God should be blessing us, not bring death into our marriage. I yelled at God. I cursed God. I hated God. I didn't even know if I believed in God anymore. I was losing my faith.

As we were going through the grieving process, a friend of mine told me to read, A New Kind of Christian, by Brian McLaren. This offering wasn't in response to what had happened, he liked the book and thought I might enjoy it too. I later read other McLaren books and can say I am not a big fan of his theology. For some strange reason though, reading this book changed the way I viewed my faith. For so long, the faith I carried with me wasn't mine. I grew up a preacher's kid. I grew up in church my whole life. My faith really belonged to my parents. It was like I inherited it.

It wasn't until I experienced a crisis of faith that I was able to get to the point where my faith became my own.

All of a sudden, I saw God differently. I saw my faith differently. I saw the outcome of the death of Kendall differently. In our pain, there was still hope. In our hurt, there was still love. In our particular situation, there was a story to be told. An opportunity to help others who experienced what we did.

Kendall may have passed away, but I believe she saved my faith. This faith crisis brought about a new kind of Christian within me. One who trusts God in the good and bad. One who has confidence that regardless of what happens, God is there. The true beauty of Kendall's story is that we get to tell it. We have helped countless other couples who have gone through something similar. I get to share my hurt and pain and bitterness, but also how my faith now is stronger because of it. It still hurts, but I realize now, God provides me comfort and I can put my faith in Him.

Kendall would have been 15 years old at the time of this writing. I still imagine what life would have been like with her. I still imagine what it would be like to be her dad: to play with her, to laugh with her, to hold her, to talk to her, to spend time with her. Those possible memories still leave sadness. However, since her passing, God has blessed us with three wonderful children. We hold them a little tighter, a little longer, because we know what loss can feel like. We talk about Kendall often with our kids. And all of us in our family know; someday we will see Kendall again. We have faith in that.

## - OUTMATCHED -

# THE ENEMY'S SCHEME

*by Nate Bush*

The slide projector clicked. The stereotypical mission presentation was underway. The missionaries were presenting for "Faith Promise Weekend." I can still hear the motor changing slides. The stereotypical missionaries wore stereotypical missionary clothing and told stereotypical missionary stories of life in the third world. I was a first world kid. I was perhaps 15 years old. Nothing they said resonated with me. I remember thinking my life was "real life," and they were speaking of some far off land which had nothing to do with my "real life." I was arrogant. I was a stereotypical first world kid thinking stereotypical first world thoughts. Nothing the missionaries spoke of was further away from my "real life" than their discussion on one particular topic - spiritual warfare.

New Mexico is not a third world country, but I do seem to spend time explaining the difference between Old Mexico and New Mexico. I planted a church in Albuquerque, New Mexico. It's still a part of the first world, although its desert landscape is often disguised in movies as a third world location. There are volcanos west of the city. You can see the whole city from them. Prior to planting, I sat on the southern most volcano and prayed. Daniel 10 is where the Spirit led me. Gabriel can't answer the prayer of Daniel because Gabriel is fighting the princes of Persia. Michael takes over the fight. Gabriel explains his delayed response to Daniel upon his arrival to answer his prayer:

FEAR NOT, DANIEL, FOR FROM THE FIRST DAY THAT YOU SET YOUR HEART TO UNDERSTAND AND HUMBLED YOURSELF BEFORE YOUR GOD, YOUR WORDS HAVE BEEN HEARD, AND I HAVE COME BECAUSE OF YOUR WORDS. THE PRINCE OF THE KINGDOM OF PERSIA WITHSTOOD ME TWENTY-ONE DAYS, BUT MICHAEL, ONE OF THE CHIEF PRINCES, CAME TO HELP ME, FOR I WAS LEFT THERE WITH THE KINGS OF PERSIA . . .
- DANIEL 10:12-14 -

I am pretty sure there is a dark prince over Albuquerque just as there was one over Persia. Perhaps there is one over your city as well.

I met with Pastor Dave after my prayer time. Dave and I had never met. On my first visit to Albuquerque I greatly appreciated Dave's church. I respected him. He graciously agreed to meet me at Satellite Coffee. There on the corner of Carlisle and Central I asked a lot of questions. Dave was patient with me. I asked Dave, "What is the enemy's scheme in Albuquerque?" Dave responded with a comparison. I was moving from Fort Lauderdale, Florida. Dave was from Albuquerque, but he had also served in ministry in Seattle, Washington. Dave said that in Fort Lauderdale and Seattle the enemy was a distractor. He said, "Satan keeps people from God with the busyness in careers and leisure activities." He continued, "In Albuquerque, Satan is an ass-kicker."

I have seen Satan's ass-kicking strategies up close and personal. My "real life" now includes some stereotypical, third-world, satanic, ass-kicking stories.

A man came in to see me. We sat down to discuss his story. He had a darkness that he could not shake. "A demon had sex with me," he revealed. He had been raped by a demon. This is not the testimony of a weird dude. This is a normal guy living in a dark place. At first I had thought Dave was speaking hyperbolically, however, I would soon realize the truth. The man who had been raped by a demon was getting his ass kicked. Every time he wanted to read the Bible, he would have an anxiety attack. He could not pray without having a severe nervous reaction. His primary feeling in life was fear. We prayed for 4 hours. We read scriptures. He proclaimed and accepted the gospel. We wept as we prayed. I believe God gave a victory that day! Soon I would start to feel the oppression of the enemy.

When I first moved to Albuquerque, I traveled a lot. Sometimes I could feel the darkness upon my return home. I do believe one day the enemy whispered to me, "Welcome back."

On the way to drop off a set of mailers, I was followed. I was really creeped out. I drove around, turning down random streets, and the car never left my tail. I finally gave up and drove to the post office downtown. As I approached the light at the post office, the car pulled up beside my passenger window. I was in my truck, so I was able to look down into the car. There were 5 guys in the car masturbating at the same time. The driver was flicking me off.

Soon after the incident at the post office, my wife started hearing voices. My kids were waking up with nightmares. I invited some friends over to have a prayer time over my house. Every night at bedtime, I started prayer walking my kids' rooms, my house, and my neighborhood. I was passionately praying against the enemy. My neighbors who eventually converted at our church, said when we moved in, "weird stuff" started happening to them.

The pastoral care needs at New City are intense. In the early days of our church, I was swamped with pastoral care needs. Weird stuff kept happening in meetings. I would feel like the Holy Spirit would say, "He is a child abuser." I would say it, and he was. I would hear the Holy Spirit say, "She is having an affair," and she was. There is a lot of generational sexual abuse here. The darkness often seems surreal.

We were renting an old real estate office for office space when we were portable. We shared the office complex with a holistic healer and massage therapist. The leasing agent whispered to me, "I am glad you guys are church people. We like a quiet office."

My first meeting in the "quiet office" was with a husband and wife. She had had an affair. The news of the affair came out in my office. I asked, "Who wants to go first?" The husband stood up. He ate a paleo diet. He was jacked from working out. When he stood, veins were popping out. His face was red. He yelled with near one-hundred percent passion, "F**K!" He yelled for a few minutes. He yelled at me. He yelled at her. There were more "F" words in that 15 minutes than in a ninety-minute Quentin Tarantino movie. I let him yell until he started throwing items in the room. I thought he was prepared to bludgeon me and his wife to death. That's when I stood up and told him to sit the "F" down. (Missionaries need to speak the language of the culture.)

After that meeting, I had a sit down with the people in our building. They had heard every word with the couple. A few weeks later, the holistic healer packed up her harp music and essential oils and moved out. The darkness of our ministry was too dark for her. There were many meetings in that office space where yelling, cursing, and occasionally door slamming took place. I have never in my life seen the darkness that I have seen in New Mexico.

I have also never seen the healing of God like I have seen in New Mexico. One couple lived in deep darkness for many years. While admitting to an affair, it was revealed the wife had a sex addiction. She would sleep with as many as three separate guys in a day. Her plan was to leave her kids and husband behind. During this time, the husband was converted in our church. I wept over them. I prayed fervently.

One day her scales dramatically fell off. It was just like Paul, a powerful and miraculous conversion. She stood up before our church and talked about the moment. God called her. She fell down to the ground and submitted everything to him. Jesus wins. When the good news about Jesus is believed, grace wins and Satan loses. This couple miraculously reconciled. The power of God's grace to confront the darkness of the enemy is awe-inspiring. The enemy tries to convince us that he is in control, but we must believe that we "are more than conquerors."

In a meeting, a man said, "You will not believe me if I told you." I said, "Bro, you have no idea." (Minutes earlier I had counseled a couple against their therapist's advice to try a threesome. I was ready for anything.) In high school, this guy was reading a Satanic book he found while skateboarding. The book caught on fire spontaneously. That same week his girlfriend broke up with him suddenly. He remembered a spell he read in the book. Burning her pictures in the backyard, he performed the spell. That night a darkness visited him. He was scared. He started dressing in all black. He was ruled by fear. The darkness spoke to him often. He was told to do things. Months later at a party a kid handed him a gun. The kid said, "Our master said to give this to you." The demonic presence wanted him to kill his girlfriend. He could not do it. He emptied the gun of the bullets, but went to her house and held the gun to her face. Then he ran. After being caught by the police, he was sentenced to house arrest. As an adult, many years later, he was struggling to believe that God was bigger than what he had done. The dark force was still kicking him in the gut and spewing lies. We prayed together over many weeks. We read the gospel together, continuously reading and praying. Recently, God freed him from the fear. The darkness left him. He is smiling again.

If I wanted to, I could pray with the demonically oppressed every day. I think Satan would be happy to overwhelm me with pastoral duties. I think this has been his scheme with me. The needs are apparent and everywhere. He wants me to get beat up trying to help all of the people that he is hurting. Satan would love it if I thought of myself as a savior.

Jesus is the only Savior. Jesus has conquered our enemy. God will soon crush Satan underneath our feet. I asked a man preparing to be baptized to tell me his story. God had been changing his life. He told me about a recent robbery attempt. This is a man with neck tattoos, a man with a drug-dealing and gang-banging past. A robber put a gun to his head. This man said to him, "Yo, kill me. I'll go to be with my savior Jesus Christ." The robber laughed and slapped him in the face. He said, "Pastor, that was when I was 'bout to stab him to death, but the Holy Spirit stopped me . . . that's why I am here to be baptized!" God is working in the dark places in Albuquerque.

Why is it so dark? I have become convinced that God led me to Daniel 10 because, like Persia in that passage, Albuquerque has a dark prince. New Mexico is a stronghold for the enemy. In New Mexico, there are 19 Native American Pueblos. There are only two who have the Bible in their own language. The Bible first arrived in the continental United States in New Mexico through Mexico. Spanish conquistadors came up from the south with Franciscan monks. The Pueblo natives had a violent reaction to the church. They revolted and killed 400 Spaniards. They drove the remaining settlers out of New Mexico. The revolt was against the theocracies being established by the Franciscan settlers. Ever since that time, there has been a violent relationship with the Gospel and New Mexico.

The Jemez Pueblo is no longer allowing Bible translators to work there. Before the project was closed, I got to know Johnny. He was translating the Bible into the Jemez language. He has since passed away. Before his passing, he told me his conversion story. He said, "When I heard the gospel in the same language that I first heard on my mother's knee, I believed it." It saddens me that everyone does not have this experience in New Mexico.

New Mexico is dark. The enemy has a stronghold. Some people are getting their asses kicked. Some people can't even hear the Bible in their own language. Yet God is on the throne saying, "Do not be afraid." The enemy always leads with fear, shame, and guilt. I am getting better at seeing this in counseling meetings. God leads with faith, grace, and forgiveness. Satan has been defeated. We are more than conquerors. The gates of hell will not prevail. The demons are bound with everlasting chains. The humble will be exalted. God is good, and He is in control. The demons shudder at the name of Jesus. There is no other name that can save. Jesus is the name above all other names. Jesus is a lamb that slays a dragon. We must not forget we are on the team with Jesus who defeated the evil forces in the heavenly realms.

I am not afraid. When I am tempted to fear, I turn to Jesus. When I see fear in the eyes of others, I turn to Jesus. When some doubt, I turn to Jesus. When anxiety strikes, I turn to Jesus. Jesus is good, and he is good at every moment of every day. Jesus is powerful. Jesus wins. He has won. He will win. Trust Jesus.

The enemy opposes every good work of the church. The enemy opposes every church planter. The enemy opposes the people whom pastors love. This battle is never won through mere hard work and dedication. This battle is won in humble prayer. This battle is never won by relying on our own strength. This battle can only be won by relying upon Christ's strength.

## - OUTMATCHED -

# CALLOUSES

*by Jason Rehmel*

I've been a pastor for nearly 15 years and I have felt ill equipped to have that title for approximately 14 years, 11 months and 29 days of it. The one day I felt equipped was my first day, when I walked into it with unabashed confidence and an unchecked ego. I remember thinking that compared to my job in the "real world," working in a church would be a cakewalk. That was the only day I ever felt that way.

Since that day almost 15 years ago, I have learned a lot and I have experienced a lot. I became a pastor because I felt I really never had a great experience when it came to church. My only approach up to that moment, which had been to complain about it, was not really working. I wanted to stop being a grumbling, complaining, armchair quarterback who was living in resentment, and start being someone who proactively could make a difference in the lives of people who were missing out on God.

In my years as a pastor, I discovered something interesting and frustrating. It was realizing that the person I had been my whole life - that person who sits back and grumbles and complains about the church and the pastors that lead it - now those were the same types of people I was going to be dealing with. I never imagined this being the case. I pictured introducing Jesus to new followers who would be hungry to learn. I didn't give any thought to the number of people who would claim a life-long relationship with Jesus, but who really lived lives very far from the life He calls us to. The hardest thing for me to deal with quickly became the presumptions life-long church members would have about who they perceived me to be and the expectations of how I was supposed to act. Here are some of the questions and statements "churched" people have asked me many, many times:

Why do you have tattoos?

Are you preaching today? I like the other guy better.

Why do you not wear a suit? (Yes. Seriously.)

We are leaving this church because _____. {INSERT ONE OF 2 MILLION SELF-INVOLVED REASONS HERE.}

Why don't you have a fish emblem on your car? (Yes. I AM TOTALLY SERIOUS.)

You drink alcohol?

How many times have you seen _____? {INSERT CHRISTIAN MOVIE TITLE HERE}? What do you mean zero?!?

On my honor, as a gentleman – every single one of those questions or statements have been asked of me...sometimes angrily. (Weirdly, the fish emblem question was being asked by one of the most agitated people I have ever talked to.)

These are the boiled-down, to-the-point, concise versions of those questions, but I've literally had them asked of me many times (well not the fish emblem one - that was a singular hilarious moment.) The reactions to my answers vary from curiosity, to amusement, to anger. Usually anger.

Long time churched people most often being the angry ones, not all, of course.

Angry, I guess, because somehow I've let them down, that I have not remained "unstained" from the world. Probably every pastor who has ever held the title 'pastor' has encountered similar questions/accusations. Those questions - or ones similar - aren't the issue. The people who ask them aren't really even the biggest problem. The biggest problem is that I have found I've started developing emotional callouses to those questions and writing the people off that ask them. Essentially, I am giving up on them. I gave up on helping them walk through their hard wiring that resists anything different than their own pre-defined notions of how things are supposed to be.

The problem with developing callouses as a pastor is that I miss opportunities to help those question askers start asking a more important question. How do we develop together more tuned-in hearts to Jesus?

In my case, my callouses form in a kind of jadedness. I start believing that those questions actually come from accusations they want to make about me condoning or promoting a life that isn't Christ-like.. I feel their expectation is that Christians need to remain completely separated from the influences of the world. So that is what they do - they separate themselves from the world. They won't watch secular movies, won't listen to secular music, won't hang out in bars, won't associate with "the lost," etc. I realize their desire to stay away from ungodly influences will help keep them "unstained," in their minds. The problem is, it will also lead them to a place that is very far from them ever getting to spend time with people who are completely outside of any kind of relationship with God.

These callouses I have developed do not allow me to help my long-churched people see what I see. Callous protection prevents me from teaching them that while living in a bubble will protect them from the corruption of a broken and lost world, it will also keep those "lost people" from experiencing God's love through them. These callouses take me dangerously close to being indifferent to people whom I want to see become fully passionate followers of Jesus.

My callouses, ironically, take me right back to where I was prior to ministry, sitting on the sidelines complaining about the state of the church and "church-people."

Here is an example. Before ministry, I worked in marketing and advertising for almost 10 years. I met a wide, diverse group of people – some were believers and others non-believers. One person I remember meeting was someone of deep faith. They had strong religious convictions and lived a very pious life. Their belief was that to remain unstained from the world they had to remain set apart from it. If conversations over lunch steered to movies, music, parties, drinking, anything deemed, "un-holy," this person would shut down. They would roll their eyes and sometimes sigh at their obvious displeasure with the content of the conversation. I have to admit – it made me feel embarrassed to be a "Christian." I was afraid everyone assumed I felt the same way, even if I wasn't making those outward kinds of expressions.

I could not imagine that one unchurched person was ever drawn closer to God or would ever have anything to do with Christianity, if this was what being a Christian looked like. I did imagine that this individual felt very good about being above that which was "un-holy." Of course, in a strange twist, my calloused self was doing the same thing to churched people. Their questions provoked the same eye-rolling, sighing and walking-away reaction from me. Was I really any better?

Where I failed with the uber-pious Christian, was not having the patience to help them understand that Super Christian is not what Jesus required of them. I failed because I wanted distance between that person and myself. Even today, I often fail as a pastor in helping uber-Christians because I just get tired of trying to turn them. I want to remind them that Jesus did not spend His time pointing out what was wrong. In fact, he hung out with the disenfranchised, the unclean, the sinful. He encouraged people, pointed out their strengths, and then led them to a better place.

I want to stay passionate about helping people see that Jesus was authentically the same – all the time. He did not change depending on the audience. He was himself in every situation. Which led to the religious elite talking badly about him.

In Luke 7:34, Jesus said that He knew what the religious elite were saying about him. He was a drunk, a glutton. All because of who He lived his life with on a daily basis. The truth is that the Pharisees who were saying these things about Jesus weren't slandering him - according to their rules, he was doing all these sinful things. Their accusations were a badge of honor. But the religious elite were missing the point.

How often today do we as Christians still focus on all the wrong things? How often today do we worry about all the wrong problems? I want to be passionate and motivated to help Christians care more about what Christ sees their life reflecting and less about what others say about their lives.

I wake up every morning energized for the folks who are far from God. That means spending time with them. In Mark 2, Jesus said, "Those who are well have no need of a physician, but those who are sick. I came not to call the righteous, but sinners.

I guarantee that this would not have been the case if Jesus spent all of his time rolling his eyes, sighing and disengaging because sinners talked about things that were unwholesome. No, Jesus and the sinners? They hung out together. The religious elite would never have joined in. No reclining at a table to drink wine and eat food with them.

I always find it amazing that Jesus never hid his activity away from the ones He knew were going to ridicule, accuse and eventually kill him. He invited them to see what He was doing. It made life harder, but it was also the only hope that any of them would ever, "get it." I don't know about you, but I find myself often just thinking it's not worth the trouble to try and influence the critics.

I want to be strong and not back down from being who God called me to be. I am reminded regularly that Jesus was harder on the religious than He was on non-believers. The whole chapter of Matthew 23 points to this. My favorite part of this story starts in verse 27:

WOE TO YOU, SCRIBES AND PHARISEES, HYPOCRITES! FOR YOU ARE LIKE WHITEWASHED TOMBS, WHICH OUTWARDLY APPEAR BEAUTIFUL, BUT WITHIN ARE FULL OF DEAD PEOPLE'S BONES AND ALL UNCLEANNESS. SO YOU ALSO OUTWARDLY APPEAR RIGHTEOUS TO OTHERS, BUT WITHIN YOU ARE FULL OF HYPOCRISY AND LAWLESSNESS.

How often do we stand on a pedestal feeling good about the things we aren't doing, while ignoring the junk that we are harboring inside: anger, bitterness, being judgmental, holding a grudge, secret sins, etc.

How do I deal with the situation when I feel those callouses developing? When I start giving up on people who have the wrong focus? When people want to spend all of their time criticizing? I spend time reading those passages I just mentioned. I remind myself that what defines me is not who they say I am or who they think I should be. What defines me is my faith in Jesus. What defines me is His calling on my life to share His Good News with those who are far from his Father. And sometimes the people who are far from Him are often the people who have been sitting in church pews their entire lives.

I love being a pastor - even a "sometimes, most of the time, ill-equipped one" who is tired and worn out some days. I love my life. I love my wife and I love my crazy kids and my two dogs and our friends and all of the fun we have together... but most of all...I love Jesus. I love the life He lived! I love the examples He set for us! I love how He interacted with people. How He loved the unloved. How he cared for the sick. How he ministered to the lonely. How He taught the self-righteous, judgmental, mean-spirited, selfish, religious-elite, time and time again with quick wit and strong words that they ultimately couldn't argue with and shouldn't have ignored. I can sometimes give up on people like that.

Everyday I have to fight those growing callouses.

## - OUTMATCHED -

# THE FIGHT WITHIN

*by Derrick Puckett*

NOT THAT I AM SPEAKING OF BEING IN NEED,
FOR I HAVE LEARNED IN WHATEVER SITUATION I AM
TO BE CONTENT. I KNOW HOW TO BE BROUGHT LOW,
AND I KNOW HOW TO ABOUND. IN ANY AND EVERY
CIRCUMSTANCE, I HAVE LEARNED THE SECRET OF
FACING PLENTY AND HUNGER, ABUNDANCE AND
NEED. I CAN DO ALL THINGS THROUGH
HIM WHO STRENGTHENS ME.
- PHILIPPIANS 4:11-13

In 2013, I entered the church planting game full of confidence and
ready with a pedigree to prove it: two plus years in a pastoral residency
program, a master's of divinity, preaching experience, pastoral experience,
and a beautiful wife who was all-in. I had read all the books and had started
and led a couple startup ministry ventures successfully. With all of this
experience, I was ready. Plus, I was going back to plant a church in the city

I loved, Chicago. We truly believed the Lord laid it upon our hearts to plant in the city. We felt we were trusting God with a vision He gave us.

The first step in planting a church is getting to know folks around the area you are planting. I met with pastors, baristas, neighbors, any human I could find. Our goal was to be students of the city. We approached the city with a clean slate. We wanted to learn as much as we could about its people and what the real needs were around each corner. Our vision was to be a multiethnic, disciple making, Gospel centered church in Chicago. The city has a long history of division at its core. We knew planting this church would be a challenge, but we also knew this church was needed.

Over our first five months in Chicago, we began holding large fellowship gatherings at our home. The purpose was to gain momentum and to foster an environment where individuals in the city could get to know one another. 40 to 50 individuals showed up every time. The church was looking very promising.

By the summer of 2014, we started doing weekly dinners called, Taco Tuesdays. We would pack out our living room with possible launch team members and eat my wife's famous fish tacos. Those Taco Tuesdays led us to preview services. By the time August rolled around, 40 people were committed to the church. With a team of 40 we launched our church on September 7, 2014. 150 people showed up that first day. Things were great! We had a great staff, people were serving and people were coming. I couldn't have asked for more as a church planter.

Then the flowery picture that was being painted began to fade. Within the first month, we had to make staff changes. At the same time, part of our core group left. A few left due to differences in expectations. Some left due to life changes. Through all of this turmoil, I unknowingly internalized what was happening. All of this took place in our first month in existence as a church.

Then month two began. One staff person quit. More of our core team left. However, seats were continuing to fill up every Sunday. Things looked great, but I felt every bit of the pain. I grew up in a single parent household. It was my mother and three younger sisters. When there were problems, I snapped into high gear to fix them. I made the the situation better and would continue to charge the hill. I was trying to do the same at our church.

We brought in three more people to join our staff. We gave them a three-month trial period to see if it was a good fit for them and for our church. For various reasons, none of them ended up staying on our staff team. Even though there was instability in our staff, the church continued to grow. People continued to jump in and serve.

But I was beginning to feel lonelier and lonelier.

I begin to feel as if I was the only one who cared about the church. I reverted back to how I grew up. I believed I had to run this church by myself. I began to feel something I had never truly felt before. I began to realize there was a deep battle going on within my soul. It was a battle between myself and God that I had never recognized before.

In my life, I had always been driven by the desire to be the best at whatever I did: playing ball at recess, getting straight A's on a report card, playing college football, or pioneering a college ministry. This drive for success I never recognized as a problem, was now a problem. Before, it was a part of me that had always been praised and honored. My go-getter mentality kept me moving forward. No problem was too big and no hill too high to climb. If anybody could make it up the hill I could. As I look back, the problem at the time was not that I had this drive deep within me. The problem was my drive was getting in the way of what God was doing in my heart.

This desire to do something great in the city of Chicago drove me. I wanted to do something people had never seen before. I would be the best preacher and pastor I could possibly be. In my mind, these were all great aspirations. I don't believe God thought they were bad. The problem was how I approached them. I approached church planting like everything else in my life - it was a sprint. Run the sprint as hard as you can. Get all the right pieces in place from the beginning. Set up the machine. Learn from the mistakes of mentors and do better. Go hard and don't give up. This mentality helped get me through everything else in my life: my parent's divorce, growing up in an impoverished area, attending a college prep high school, going to college, playing college football, and getting a master's degree. All I knew was to do things at the highest level possible and let nothing get me down.

The issue at hand was that I had no idea this was a problem. This was normal for me.

Here we were, four months into our church plant, and I was depressed. I could not put words to what I was feeling. God was pruning my heart in unexplainable ways. I found out I harbored deep distrust issues with Him. I started to realize the reason I did everything at such a high level, all the time, was because of trust issues with God. I never knew these existed, until now.

I did not realize it at the time, but the Lord was trying to teach me to trust Him; which was hard, because I thought I did. The indication of my distrust came when things happened at the church that seemed like a failure, and I never went to the Lord to consult Him. I snapped into figure-it-out mode and tried to fix it, and every time I made a decision, it seemed like I fell on my face.

See, the will to make things work, the will to charge the hill, the determination to do things at the highest level possible, were all great characteristics to have as a church planter, but I was learning the hard way, that none of those are the number one characteristic. The number 1 characteristic was to have faith, and trust God with what He was doing with His church, but also in my heart. This was very convicting. The most convicting part about it was that I am a pastor. I was supposed to already believe in this, and I thought I did.

We were early in the life of our church plant and I thought I was trusting God. Come to find out, it was not trust at all.

The wrestling match had begun. I learned how to wrestle with how God wired me. At the same time, I learned to trust Him. For so long, I carried the burden of the church and my life on my shoulders. My experiences in life brought me to this place of distrust. I carried the weight of being the only male in a house full of women. I needed to be the man-of-the-house.

I carried the weight of succeeding as a black man without a father around. I carried the weight of being a great athlete and student in a world where black men don't do both. I carried the weight of having a great marriage and providing for my family when it was something I had never experienced. I carried all of this burden on my shoulders. I never truly learned how to trust anyone. Until I starting walking with God.

However, I really began to understand how to trust God by planting this church. Jesus was making sure I knew He was God and I could trust Him.

This wasn't a simple change in my life. This wrestling match was hard because I felt God was killing something in me that made me who I was. It was all I knew. For God to be prodding at my identity in this way was paralyzing. I had no idea what to do or how to move forward. I was learning a hard lesson, one I preached on many times, but I'm not sure I really listened.

I was learning my identity didn't come from my doing or my work ethic, but that it came from God. This meant that even if I failed doing something to the best of my ability, my identity would not change because God is unchanging. Even if I succeeded, my identity isn't in the success because Jesus already accomplished everything on the cross.

The wonderful world of church planting - where I felt I was there to help everyone else - was exposing idols in my heart at a depth I had never dove to before. Remember, the church is God's bride. It is not another classroom to get an A in. It is not another football game to try and score a touchdown. It is not trying to overcome the odds as a black man with the world seemingly against him.

The church is the reason He went to the cross. His love for His bride is what made Him step out of heaven, come down to earth and allow Himself to be hung on a cross. The Lord was trying to teach me that in order for this church plant to work, it had to have nothing to do with my vision, or anything I brought to the table. The success would come in Christ's shed blood on the cross, that's the vision. That's all the world needed to be done. For this church plant to be successful, I needed to not just preach the cross, but believe it with every ounce of my being. God was trying to point out that this church was only going to happen because of Him, not me.

We are a year and a half into our church plant and things are going well. The church is continually growing. I am personally doing well. I finally realized God was not trying to kill how He made me. He made me in His image. He allowed me to experience certain things to prepare me for what He would do with me. Yet none of my experiences defined me. My identity is in Christ. In order to do anything according to his will and purpose, I had to trust Him. No matter what the outcome may be. I began to understand that God knows what He wants to accomplish. I was okay not controlling the outcome. Everyday, I approach my work knowing I am working to the glory of God. Ultimately, it is not me doing the work, but Him doing a work through me. In that truth I find myself content and at peace in all things, because it is not in my hands, but His.

## - OUTMATCHED -

# PRIDE AND FAITHFULNESS

*by Danny Schaffner, Jr.*

I never really planned on being a church planter. I grew up in small to medium-sized churches throughout the Midwest. Deciding to follow in the path of my family only came after a hard fought battle with God to determine whether or not to "professionally" serve Jesus.

After about 15 years in student ministry - and chances to serve is some growing, dynamic churches - I jumped head-first, wide-eyed and idealistic to a fault, into the call to plant a church.

At the time, I was serving at a church that I deeply loved. I grew a lot in my time there. However, the longer I was there, the more I realized I wanted to lead and preach. Two friends of mine, Bart Stone and Scott Hatfield, challenged me to consider doing something I had never desired. Both of them were jumping into the world of church planting and thought I should do the same.

Scott knew of a church in an urban area that wanted to flip the church. Yep, kind of like flipping houses. I felt I would be a good fit. I knew I loved doing ministry in urban settings. All I wanted was to find a people I could love and lead. We would then see what God might do through all of us.

So...Tampa, Florida was my calling, the 33603. A church had closed its doors and left her assets to do a new work. This was a zip code, predominantly Latino, secondarily African American, and then Caucasian, that represented the general demographics that our nation will represent in the next decade or two. Every tribe, tongue, and nation was well represented in our community. And it was all very different than what this white, meat and potatoes, built-for-hibernation cold, Iowa-winters guy was used to.

For the first time in my life, I was choosing to be the minority - ethnically, spiritually, and economically. What was normal to me was not normal to others. Conversations, customs, family routines, everything around me was both foreign and an adventure. Work, school, and play, even your local Walmart, bore the marking of multi-culturalism. A whole new style of life in ministry opened up to me. It reminded me that before Jesus ever said, "Go into all the world," he said, "Love your neighbor as yourself." I was now living in a world that spoke globally and lived local. Going into all the world meant serving from my own backyard.

So I began to build a team. No, I began to build a dream team. I wanted this team to reflect our community. I hired a young Caucasian lady from my last student ministry who had the artistic vision of her mom and the executive leadership detail of her dad. She was to be our Children's Pastor and Ministry Administrator. We hired a young, African American man from the urban center of Louisville. We met in a chance passing at a convention. He had military in his background, college football on his resume, and worked ministry in the inner city. He would oversee all things involving Community Impact. We hired a young Latino man from Honduras. He is a pastor's pastor. He was a gentle voice from the pulpit, compassionate for people and steady in his work ethic. He was to be our

Groups Pastor. Finally, we hired a local friend from the other side of the Bay. He was from St. Petersburg and had grown up a true Florida boy. He was to lead our Creative Arts team. I was Lead Pastor in charge of vision, fundraising, preaching, and whatever else needed to get done.

We all moved to Tampa. We had a place to meet for worship services, but we needed to prep, clean up, and remodel the facility. We recruited mission teams from the midwest and student ministry friends who wanted "warm mission trips," in early spring.

We began to assess the needs of our community. It was a mess. Tampa was financially struggling. We began our project when the recession hit and the financial bubble burst. The public schools were broken. The school where my youngest boys attended had only 16 out of almost 400 students who could afford the daily school lunch. My boys were two of the 16. Tampa was very irreligious, even though there seemed to be some representation of spirituality on every corner - good or bad. It was completely unlike the Bible belt. Everyone said they went to church - even if they didn't.

With my dream team intact and plan of attack in place, we started getting to know Tampa. We began by visiting churches to see who they were and made sure we were unique. Tampa has an incredible variety of churches. Crossover Community Church, Relevant Church, Church @ the Bay, Church of the Suncoast and Grace Family Church all impacted us in some way. This group of churches invested in me and our church in ways many people will never know. They supported us, prayed for us, encouraged us, shared ideas with us, and cheered us on. I will be forever be grateful for their generosity.

Our church began partnerships with local schools. We gave out backpacks to help under resourced families. We did multiple facets of servant evangelism; we gave out free water bottles at busy intersections and handed out Krispy Kreme donuts to local businesses. We prayer walked our community. We hung door hangers as invitations for neighbors to attend.

We sent out invites through postcards. We held Backyard BBQ's. If it was in a church planting book, we tried it.

September 9, 2007, Launch Day. We held two services that morning and 255 people showed up. Our supporting church planting organizations: Stadia and Florida Church Partners were there to see their baby born. Neighbors showed up to check us out. We had a full children's ministry from day one. The band led worship and even did a John Mayer cover, "Waiting On The World To Change." My message that day was about how we cannot wait on the world to change because God called us to change the world with him. We did announcements in English and Spanish. Our team nailed the day. So, there we were: launched, living, and now it was time to be who we said we were.

Like a young man with his first car, I was ready to take this church out for a spin. With the windows down and my mullet blowing in the wind - so to speak - I was the proud pastor of a newly launched church. I was proud of her. I had crafted what I thought was the perfect mission and vision statement. It was relationally focused and strategically accurate. I crafted values that caught the heart of our church and not just the path of maturity. I was so proud. Did I mention that? What is it scripture says?

Oh yeah,

GOD OPPOSES THE PROUD, BUT SHOWS
FAVOR TO THE HUMBLE.
- 1 PETER 5:5B -

There is this saying, "Pride comes before the fall." I need you to know this is most definitely true. Let me share what happened.

A couple weeks after we launched, our church planting management team had an emergency meeting. Seems we were spending more money than we had approved to mobilize. So what was the emergency meeting about? Is this fixable? Can the church stay open? Do we keep me at the helm? Fortunately the answers to all of the questions were yes, but this wasn't our last issue.

By October, we saw our attendance cut in half from our launch date numbers. In November, a staff member and I got 'sideways' and we let him go. That same month, thieves gutted our A/C units for copper and we had to get those fixed. In December, another staff member came to me and said his marriage was on the rocks and he needed to leave.

In the days, months and years to come, here is what we experienced...

- We lost another staff member due to personal conflict.

- My mother-in-law would be diagnosed with cancer.

- We removed one of my children from our home to place them in a children's home.

- The church barely made payroll.

- The needs of our community outweighed the provision of our people.

- We had individuals try and steal the purses of our members on Sunday morning.

- My mother-in-law succumbed to cancer.

- My wife endured deep depression.

- My marriage had mostly become a partnership for ministry because the emotional price was so high.

In the midst of all of this, I was invited by leaders I respected to one of those major, "Who's Who" gatherings in California. The group included mostly men under 40 who were supposedly the next crew of real influencers. I remember being asked by the guys there, "What's it like planting in Florida?"

I replied, "It's like getting up every morning and getting your butt handed to you."

"No really, dude. You're in *Tampa* right?"

"Yes, really, dude. Every day," I said.

Later at the same retreat, we were asked what really matters and what really makes a difference. A few said great things like, "Love your people. Preach well. Trust God." My tank was empty. Frankly, I was embarrassed. These are the words which left my lips, "I have learned that I drink too often from the fountain of success, but God has called us to really only drink from the fountain of faithfulness."

There it was. The confession of my pitiful soul. I am but a man in ministry, following a God who took on the very nature of a servant. Why do I long for something greater than He?

I caught up with my mentor, Hal Mayer. He said "So what if you are who people said you are? What if all your faults are true? Whether you can change it or not doesn't matter. What matters is, did God call you to Tampa?"

"Yeah, I do feel called," I answered.

"Then all God requires of you is to answer the calling and be faithful," Hal responded. (This was only three months after launching our church.)

I began to think about the moments God had been faithful to me and God's church.

On one occasion, I served at a senior high week of church camp near Las Vegas, Nevada. I was the missionary for the week and found out by e-mail we were not going to make payroll in our first summer. 200 kids and adults gave over $10,000 and we never came close to broke again.

The work of planting this church was not simply about planting a church. It was about following God. It was about forging me into Christ's likeness. It felt like I was Eustace, the rotten kid in the C.S. Lewis writings that becomes a dragon. I needed Aslan the lion to help remove the scales of my pride no matter how painful it may be. Aslan/Jesus undressed me of myself. Man, I loved me some me. It was painful, but for the first time, I realized who I was truly meant to be.

When I began to feel overwhelmed and underqualified, I thought of Moses. God called Moses back to faithfulness.

When I began to see my weaknesses and temptations, I thought of David. God called David back to faithfulness.

When I saw my personal failures and denials, I thought of Peter. Guess what God did? God called him back to faithfulness.

Over time, we found real traction in our urban corridor. At our peak, over 200 people showed up every Sunday. We baptized over 80 people in a little more than six years. We built key friendships I can never replace, nor mention in this story, but you know who you are. God did an incredible work in that church. I am forever in debt to having the honor of being many of those individual's first pastor.

After several hard years, our family came to a time of evaluation. I entered a four-week period of prayer with my wife. Should we stay? Not for a year, but for good. Or was there some place else we should consider? We invited key people into our lives to pray with us. I invited thirteen friends to pray for us and to share their advice. I met with people who knew me and discussed my strengths and weaknesses. We listened and waited.

After four weeks, I looked at my wife and said, "Hey, I was talking to Kent and he thinks we either need to root in and make Tampa our home, or this is the time to go." We chatted and thought. I knew I had nothing more to give. I had tried all I could and held no more ideas. My wife felt the same way. I looked at her and said, "I feel released. I don't know what this means, but it is as if God is saying it is ok to let go."

The chance to plant a church in Florida sounded very appealing - especially in Tampa. Beaches, amusement parks, a zoo, and the sun. These amenities are often what people think about when they think about Tampa. To me, it will never be about that. It will always be the place where God stripped me of me and planted a church. Tampa is about the lives that He changed. Specifically mine.

I experienced how hard church planting can be. I am often asked, "Would you ever plant a church again?" I pray my answer will always be, "If God asks me to."

## - OUTMATCHED -

# ALL ALONE

### *by Nate Bush*

I love to network. If networking is a spiritual gift, I probably have it. Connecting people to each other and to great ideas makes me smile. I really get the greatest joy in spinning ideas and watching them take flight with people who love working with those ideas in community. If networking is one of my greatest joys, working alone is one of my greatest pains.

I often get asked, "What organizations are a part of your network?" In other words, "What church planting groups partnered with you to plant your church?" It's a hard question to answer. There was not a strong network in New Mexico. So, to plant New City Church we needed other organizations to partner with us. Several groups gave to our local network, although the local network was the only partner that claimed our church plant as their own.

Sadly, after we planted, a theological debate over baptism ensued. The lead network walked away. Not even two years old, we were all alone. This made me very sad.

Some people refer to our church plant as a "parachute plant." This is a military term. It sounds brave and noble. Parachuting behind enemy lines is an extra-ordinary act. Unless a community is so remote that only a parachuter can get to it through an extra-ordinary way, it's probably unwise to parachute in. There is nothing wrong with an ordinary act of church planting. An ordinary act would include planting with a team of people who already know and love the community.

I am not an extra-ordinary church planter. I have been humbled in my work. Humble enough to tell you my story is all about Jesus and his church and not about me.

Loneliness in ministry is painful. Our first service was on Easter of 2010. At the end of 2010 we had a major financial crisis. When the financial crisis struck, I had no network to lean on. It felt like no one cared. My dream and calling looked like it was going to fail. I was working my ass off. I needed community, but compassion was nowhere to be found. I remember praying, "Lord, I am desperate for some encouragement." There are few feelings as desperate as opening your inbox hoping there would be an email of encouragement or going to the post office box hoping there would be a surprise gift waiting for you, and finding nothing.

Our trailer was stolen in 2012. We locked it up in a local church parking lot. In 2013 our trailer was stolen again. We had moved the trailer to a lot with barbed wire fencing and video surveillance. Barbed wire and surveillance did not deter the thieves. Again, I heard crickets from our networks.

The 2013 theft incident was really bad. It was country music bad. I lost my dog in the mountains on Saturday night, literally. It was late and the roads were icing up. I had to leave my dog overnight in the mountains. As soon as church was over on Sunday, I hooked up my camper and headed to the mountains to find my dog. It was snowy, really snowy. I found my dog. I got stuck in the snow. I lost my dog again. I found my dog two hours later. I got unstuck with the help of a wench I borrowed from a kind passerby on a road about a mile from where I was stuck. On the way down the mountain, my dog puked all over my truck. As soon as I got back into cell range, my phone lit up with messages informing me the trailer had been stolen, again.

God is at work right now redeeming a broken world. He is redeeming my broken church planting story. My lack of a church planting network created a deep desire in me to build a personal network with pastors in our city. I held conferences for pastors. I brought in guest speakers. I held special lunches and network meetings.

There was a phrase I kept hearing, "I am glad you're doing this, but pastors in this city don't work together." I have since discovered this was a Satanic lie that pastors were believing.

By the time the second trailer was stolen, several local churches from various tribes came to our assistance. A local Baptist church plant in prelaunch phase came over to set up their equipment for us. The weekend after our theft, our set-up team had the Sunday off! Another local nondenominational Reformed church let us borrow equipment the following week. A local Assemblies of God church called and offered prayers over our space and any equipment we might need. A local Anglican pastor reached out and offered services and prayed for me. There were dozens of churches from various backgrounds that came to our aid.

I started saying things like, "I am blessed to be one pastor among many great pastors in our city." An unquenchable affection for the local church begin to develop in me. We already began reframing the question, "How can we be the best church in the city?" to "How can we be the best church for the city?" It was clear to me. God was calling me to lead New City in such a way that we brought the local church together.

Every year, New City Church gives away her Easter offering. One year we committed $20,000 to Mission Avenue Elementary School. There we sat with Principal Garcia and listened to her dream about how the money might be used. She dreamed of a club we later called Shine Club. Shine

Club had a great first year. We saw the school progress from a D school to a B school. The club started to get a positive reputation among Albuquerque Public School district officials. APS is the largest school district in New Mexico. Roughly half of New Mexican children attend an APS school. We hired a dynamic staff person, Lisa Fuller, to lead this initiative.

Shine Club is now the Shine Partnership because it encompasses much more than just an after-school club. Shine's secret sauce is facilitating a sit down between pastors and principals. Shine facilitates an innovation that a particular school and church can create to better serve the common good, namely children in our state. Under Lisa's leadership, Shine has become one of the most significant church partnerships in our city. In the spring of 2016, we hosted an event with over a hundred APS officials and local pastors together. Shine is pairing dozens of schools and churches in partnership. APS has offered Shine a Memorandum of Understanding anointing Shine as the primary organization approved of by APS to connect churches and schools. Now whenever a church approaches a school, they are referred to Shine. Shine trains churches and pairs them with schools in need. New Mexico in 2016 was ranked 49th in education in America. The Kids' Count Report listed New Mexico as, "the worst state to be a child." Now New City Church - through Shine - is working out God's redemption plan for our city.

In addition to Shine, we started a youth ministry for churches in our city. It was clear there were a number of smaller churches struggling to reach parents of middle school and high school students. To be a service to our city, we started The Collective. Over one hundred students are regularly involved in The Collective. We have 15 churches and 7 denominations participating. The responsibilities are shared between student pastors and pastors of churches. Everyone participates. Churches who can afford it give towards events. The Collective meets once a month for a fun event. The gospel is shared every time. Students are responding to the gospel and lives are changing. I am really blessed to be one of the pastors in Albuquerque.

Recently, pastors from four different denominations have been gathering and dreaming. I think God is building a new church planting network. We are dreaming of a network that does street-level training, provides financial support, and facilitates justice work in our state. We are going to launch this new network in 2016.

Our pilot project is a Spanish speaking church plant that launched Easter Sunday 2016. Abiel Diaz is the church planter. Abiel has been my apprentice leader for 18 months. He and his wife Emily attended two assessments and passed both. Their church, appropriately named, is Cuidad de Gracia or City of Grace. This new church is being supported by Baptist, Anglican, Presbyterian, Evangelical Free, and non-denominational churches in town. These churches have already ponied up and are showing we are better together. If you asked any of the pastors of the supporting churches they would say, "I am really blessed to be one of the pastors in my city."

I am saddened by our earlier story. There is much in my story to gripe about. As I look back over our time here in New Mexico, I wonder if any of what is happening within our city today would have happened without my sad story?

I am smiling a lot lately. I am glad God is redeeming my broken story. I am really excited about what God is up to in our city. I have to keep working at moving myself out of the center. I am thankful for God's faithfulness. Without God's constant steadfast love, I might start thinking I need to be the savior. I have been humbled by what God has done. Jesus is the hero of our story. Jesus is building a network of pastors in my city. I never worry anymore about being alone.

# ON THE ROPES

## AND IN TROUBLE

### ROUND TWO

- ON THE ROPES -

# WHAT I WOULD TELL CHURCH PLANTERS

*by Aaron M. Brockett*

Six months after the grand opening of our church plant, I hit a wall. The combination of seeing the last of the "well-wishers" depart, watching our first disillusioned family leave the church, and experiencing the drought of summer attendance was too much. I'd given everything I had to get this young church started and now with the needle of my emotional tank firmly planted on "empty," I wanted to bail. To be honest, I was irritated with the stories of 'church planters turned mega-church pastors' that made it look so easy (or so I thought). On paper, we'd done everything we were supposed to do. We had hit our marks, raised the funds, developed a launch team, and I was preaching my guts out. The results, from my perspective, weren't matching the effort we were investing.

That's right around the time when I received a phone call from the search committee of one of those mega-churches looking for a new lead pastor. I'm not sure why my wife, Lindsay and I decided to drive down one weekend for a visit. We knew there was no way we could leave our church plant when it was only six months old. Looking back, I think we were lonely enough that a weekend away together sounded really, really good. So we went. And we were tempted to take the job. Man, were we tempted. All right, I was more tempted than she was. I kept thinking, "If I only had this facility…this staff…these elders…these people, then ministry would be so fruitful and fulfilling." Everything within me tried to figure out a way to make it feel as if God were calling us away from the church plant and into a mega-church. You know, this role fits my gifts better. Maybe God used the last six months to prepare me for another challenge. Paul didn't stay at any of the churches he planted very long - now I know why!

I can spiritualize cowardice with the best of them, but it was to no avail. God wouldn't let us go and I wasn't very happy about it. I couldn't believe I was hearing myself tell that search team, "No, we're going to stay" as I hung up the phone.

For the next four years, we labored to establish that young church all the while looking out at the "mega-boys" in the big churches around the country with a bit of disdain. Their success made me feel like a loser at times. I know, it wasn't healthy and I was aware of it, but that didn't make the feelings any less real. I actually grew somewhat disenfranchised with the large church as a result. We gave the church plant all that we had and God worked in and through the lives of people, one at a time. As it turns out, my heart needed those challenging years more than God needed me to plant a church.

Several years later, through a series of unexpected events, I found myself following a well-loved, long-tenured pastor at one of those mega-churches that I'd looked upon with suspicion and envy from a distance. We weren't looking for the opportunity; God led us to it. I went from leading a church plant of 125 people, to leading a church of 1,600 within the span of a year and a half. It felt a bit like jumping onto a speeding Amtrak train. I really had no idea what I was doing and was thrown into a steep learning curve. And yet, by God's grace the church has grown rapidly over the past eight years to multiple campuses.

It has been unreal and even perplexing at times. Before you get all uptight thinking this is just another piece on, "How You Too, Can Grow A Mega-Church!" calm down. Seriously. Relax. Ask anyone who knows me well and they'll tell you that I'm not a hard-driving, ambitious, type-A kind of guy. In fact, most people get annoyed with me because I'm too quiet (geesh, extroverts drive me crazy!). The reason why I mention this is because a couple of years ago a friend of mine who helps to plant churches asked me this question, "So Aaron, what are you doing now that's different from what you did then?"

Honestly, I'd never really stopped to consider that question. From his perspective, I had to be doing something different from the days of being a struggling church planter in order to be experiencing this kind of growth in a mega church. Here was my honest answer: "I have no idea."

Now, what I meant wasn't that I was walking around the hallways of the church like a bumbling idiot completely clueless as to what I'm doing (although I'm sure there are some days my staff and others in our church would say that description sounds about right). What I meant was that there hadn't been a day where I declared, "I'm going to change this and that about the way I'm leading," and then when I did, our church really took off.

There wasn't a formula, conference, or book that changed anything. Don't hear me say that I'm opposed to any of those. I have certainly grown from each of those tools and experiences. I'm just saying, "There was no secret sauce."

Serving a small, struggling church plant as well as serving a growing mega-church has taught me more about 1 Corinthians 3:6-9 than any particular method of ministry or leadership philosophy.

I PLANTED, APOLLOS WATERED, BUT GOD GAVE THE
GROWTH. SO NEITHER HE WHO PLANTS NOR HE WHO
WATERS IS ANYTHING, BUT ONLY GOD WHO GIVES THE
GROWTH. HE WHO PLANTS AND HE WHO WATERS ARE
ONE, AND EACH WILL RECEIVE HIS WAGES ACCORDING
TO HIS LABOR. FOR WE ARE GOD'S FELLOW WORKERS.
YOU ARE GOD'S FIELD, GOD'S BUILDING.
- 1 CORINTHIANS 3:6-9 -

This passage means more to me than it ever has because I've been both a 'planter' and a 'waterer.' Hear me church planter, the community or culture you are ministering in is the soil, the seed is the gospel, and God is the one orchestrating the growth (or lack thereof). "Growth" isn't always linked to numerical increase, but instead to the myriad of ways that God desires to grow us as His people. This picture should be incredibly humbling and freeing to those of us who have the honor of leading a local church (whether it's mega, mini, or anywhere in between). So with that backdrop, this is what I would tell church planters and it probably applies to you too, whoever you are:

Be careful not to assign moral value to the size of a church. This is an easy thing to do. People have strong opinions about the "right" size a church should be, whatever that means. The truth is that some churches are small because there isn't enough love, the vision is unclear, and the systems are unhealthy. And others are big, because they are over-hyped and over-accommodating to culture. However, this isn't true for every small or big church! In the New Testament, the church in Corinth appears relatively small and the church in Jerusalem grew quite large. Size isn't spiritual. It's a by-product of a variety of factors, many of which we simply have no control over. It is a sin to generate numerical growth for anyone's glory other than Jesus, but it is a equally grievous sin to limit or discourage numerical growth due to our own comfort or bias. After serving in both small and big churches, there are strengths and weaknesses to both. There are opportunities and limitations with each. Dr. Sam Chand, in his book,

"Leadership Pain," says that growth comes as our threshold for pain as a leader increases.

So yeah, nobody told me about that, but it's so true. As a church planter, you are planting the seed of the gospel within the community you serve. Focus on knowing Jesus and making him known and leave the results up to Him.

The Church will prevail, not the particular style of church we prefer in the moment. French emperor Napoleon Bonaparte once said that the best way to understand someone is to discover what was happening in the world when they were twenty years old. There is a lot of sobering truth in that statement. It amazes me how much "friendly fire" there is to endure within ministry today. By no means am I saying we cannot or should not learn from the thoughtful, direct, yet redemptive critique of other godly men and women. I'm just saying that if we aren't careful, the conversation can degenerate into a tone that indicates we are more interested in winning the debate than advancing the Kingdom.

When Jesus told Peter that the Church would prevail He didn't put any adjectives in front of it. It wasn't the small church, the big church, the rockin church, or the simple church. The type of church that pleases God is the one who receives people as they are, removes all unnecessary barriers that keep those people from Jesus, and points them towards the truth of God's Word which delivers all of us from death to life. Since the Church is Jesus' bride and not yours (Rev. 2-3), let Him deal with her imperfections, inconsistencies, and flaws. He's been looking at her without her makeup on for 2,000 years already! He doesn't need you or me pointing out that nasty mole on the back of her neck. He'll deal with it. I don't care what style of church you prefer. Just make sure that in your gathering: Jesus is the focus, your Bible is open, and the gospel narrative is your refrain. And don't be surprised if God decides to bless that gathering with growth - then you can deal with your own critics.

Recognize that Jesus is the true lead pastor of your church. I love that we are reminded in 1 Peter that Jesus is our Chief Shepherd. One common mistake I've made and seen others make is that when it comes to ministry, we have a tendency to take ourselves too seriously and Jesus not seriously enough. We never set out to do this intentionally, it just happens when criticism comes our way, when there is interpersonal conflict with someone on our staff, or the pressure to succeed presses in on us as we give in to the temptation to compare our ministry with someone else's. It's been helpful for me in those vulnerable moments, to remember the way Jesus looks upon my feeble service to Him in His Church.

Every year for the past five years, I've taken my son Conor out to Colorado for two or three days of snow skiing. I didn't learn to ski until I was in college, so I made a decision a long time ago that I would teach him when he was young. He's 13 now, but when we started taking these trips five years ago it was rough. He complained about everything, and we hadn't even gotten him into his ski boots yet! In those early trips he fell constantly, got tired easily, and gave up about a million times. This past year, however, I noticed how much he had improved. I'm still a bit faster than he is, but not by much. He kept up with me on every run, never complained, and I got tired long before he did. At one point, we found ourselves at the top of a black diamond run (for those of you who don't ski, this is for expert skiers only). I took a look and thought he could handle it, but chose not to tell him it was black diamond so it wouldn't mess with his head. We started off and he followed me all the way down. At the bottom, I looked over at him and said, "Congratulations buddy, you just did your first black diamond!" His response and facial expression was priceless. He said, "No way!" turning around to take another look with pride and disbelief. It was an awesome moment.

Church planting can be rough...like really rough...there will be times it will feel like you're on the ground flat on your back more than taking ground on your feet. Get back up, keep going, and stay close to Jesus. What he wants for you is something far better than the momentary "success" of your church plant. He is refining your heart, maturing your leadership, and preparing you for what's next; that process almost always involves pain, but that pain comes with great reward. When you realize that Jesus cares more about the condition of your eternal soul than the "success" of your temporary church, it is a freeing reality that sets you up for years of fruitful service for the Kingdom, regardless of your circumstances. Plant relentlessly. Water faithfully. Then go take a nap. I am.

- ON THE ROPES -

# WHEN THE LEVEE BREAKS

*by Derek Sweatman*

*If it keeps on rainin', levee's goin' to break*
*If it keeps on rainin', levee's goin' to break*
*And when the levee breaks I'll have no place to stay*
**Kansas Joe McCoy & Memphis Minnie**
When The Levee Breaks (1929)

She talked, I listened.

That's about all you can do when someone is leaving the church. These conversations don't come with reversals, only endings. People don't usually go in a fit of rage. Some do, yes. But most don't. Most go slowly, over time. For weeks or months or even years, they work up the courage to cut loose. It's a slow fade. It's the worst kind of breakup. And the whole time she was giving me the reasons why she and her family were moving on, all I could think about was how in the hell I was going to get into their home to get my INXS cassette tape back. Live Baby, Live, 1991. Gone forever.

I left the office for the rest of the day after that phone call. We're a small shop. We all work in the same room. I didn't want to be consoled, or fixed, or made to feel guilty with some quote from Galatians about pleasing God over people. I wanted to drink. A lot. But I don't drink. Not anymore. So I went home. I stood there and stared at the Jerry Garcia poster on our kitchen wall, happy that my wife is the kind who lets that kind of thing hang on our wall. Jerry is gone. Died in 1995. I'm still around. So I had that going for me.

I don't mean to sound flippant. I'm not. It's just that that kind of shit had been rolling in at a steady pace for so long that it had become the kind of thing I had grown to expect. Two weeks after that phone call, I got another one from our landlord (we lease our space) who told me we had 60 days to get out. The property had been sold, and the developers wanted to get started straightaway. It's one thing to move a family in two months. It's another to move a congregation. Two weeks after that? I had to let a part-time staff member go.

I was on the ropes.

That's the phrase for when you're cornered and unable to get clear of what's happening to you. It's that feeling of being trapped in a blur of opposition, and with no foreseeable escape. You can't move out of the way of the hits, and the hits keep coming. In boxing, it's a literal station. You're pressed up against the ropes that frame the ring, and your competitor has you contained, hitting you over and over and over again. You've seen it before. The guy on the ropes just covers his head and tries to lean far enough forward to change the situation. Sometimes it works. Sometimes he goes down.

There had been times over the last year when I just wanted to fall to the floor. That way the hits would have stopped, at least long enough for me to crawl out of the way. But when you're on the ropes, you can't go anywhere.

70

I had tried to quit.

Twice.

Two churches reached out to me, and I applied to them both. In the end, they both said no. From the start I wasn't really interested in going. Those were just short-term opportunities to feel needed, in control, and to escape my current situation, if only in my mind. But a rejection is still a rejection. And nothing makes your current situation seem worse than when your potential way out closes up.

Those rejections temporarily escalated my awareness of everything that was falling apart on my watch. Attendance was dropping. The finances weren't improving. People were leaving. Small groups were folding. Marriages were breaking. People weren't singing. Preaching was flattening. Classes weren't getting off the ground. Events weren't connecting. And I was more aware than ever of how our baptistery, like those empty and hollowed out cisterns at the wedding at Cana, just sat there, invisible like, and unused (except for hiding guitar cases on Sunday). It got to the point where I would walk in on Monday fully expecting to chart another loss by Friday.

I was on the ropes.

Depression is not an easy thing. It takes over in weird ways. I kept showering, and I didn't stop eating. But I did disappear a lot. I would tell my staff team that I was headed home to work for the rest of the day, to work in quiet on my sermon or something. It was all a lie. I would go home mid-morning and sleep for the rest of the day. Sometimes two or three times a week this would happen.

I met with a pastor in another city. We both teach a course at the same university. He had become a friend of trust and encouragement. He had also been through all this himself. He was older. That's key. Two pastors who are the same age are almost useless in mutual counseling. You need someone ahead of you, someone with scars from cuts that you're only just receiving. He asked me if I was sleeping all day. I said I was. He asked if I was tired of living. I said no. He asked if I was seeing a counselor. I said it had been awhile. He stared at me. I said I would make the phone call. I said that I just needed a win, for something to go in the right direction.

The weird thing was this: despite all that was going in the wrong direction, there were things going in the right direction. Yes, it was a long season of watching people move on, of things not working out financially, of ministry initiatives not getting off the ground, all of which led to a feeling of scarcity among the staff and leaders. But in the midst of all that, there were continuous displays of God's presence among us, and of His dedicated work in and through us.

It helps when you take a rotation in serving the communion. In our services everyone comes forward to receive the bread and the juice. We speak to those who are served, "The body of Christ, broken for you; the blood of Christ, poured out for you." If we know their names, we add those in: "Janet, the body of Christ, broken for you." To say those words while looking into the eyes of someone has done more for me than I can explain here. To say those words to the addict, the divorcee, the couple that's on the brink, the childless, the depressed, the guilt-ridden, the scared, the doubtful, the agnostic, and the people who never seem to wander from the Lord...it's all too much to take in in 5 minutes. I often cry as a server of the communion, but just enough that I can still speak, still smile, and still hold up the line while I hug the person.

In 1 Timothy 4:12, Paul writes:

LET NO ONE LOOK DOWN ON YOU FOR YOUR YOUTH, BUT SET THE AN EXAMPLE FOR BELIEVERS IN SPEECH, IN CONDUCT, IN LOVE, IN FAITH, IN PURITY.

The word for "example" here is typos (τύπος), a word that describes the aftermath of opposition. It means the "mark" of a hit or cut. Thomas used the same word when he announced his disbelief in the resurrection, saying,

UNLESS I SEE IN HIS HANDS THE TYPOS OF THE NAILS,
AND PLACE MY HAND INTO HIS SIDE,
I WILL NEVER BELIEVE.
- JOHN 20:25 -

Timothy wanted to walk away from that pastoral gig in Ephesus. Paul wanted him to stay. There was still work to be done, and Timothy needed to sit tight and work it through. He was apparently under a great deal of stress, and it was coming from his own people, the result of his own work. I appreciate that Paul didn't impose a possible leadership issue on Timothy's part, but rather a call to consider what ministry was doing to him, not for him (or for his church).

Ministry will always leave a mark. It's not possible to go through this unscathed. Scars, and the stories behind them, are to be expected. Even embraced. But it seems that we have the choice in the kind of mark ministry leaves on us. Look at that list again: the mark of speech, of conduct, of love, of faith, of purity. (And can we just agree on the genius of the sequence of this list? Isn't it always the case that when we're under a lot of negative pressure that the first thing to go is our speech? Which can open the door to destructive conduct. Which can erode our love. Which can bring conflict into our faith. Which can erase our calling to be set apart.)

We have the choice of the kind of mark ministry will leave on us.

Ministry is a sobering vocation, and must be embraced as such. Its leader is to stand on his own two feet, tall in the midst of whatever comes his way, unwilling to bury and hide the troubles underneath escapist behaviors. Ministry must be allowed to hit, and to hit hard. The velocity of suffering and pain and anger and doubt and confusion and insecurity is enough to leave one in the valley of the shadow of death, stunned and uncertain. But do not run.

Stand still.

Encircled.

Afraid.

Desperate.

Inadequate.

It is here reliance emerges. The Lord again becomes the guide, the way through, and the way out. Resurrection begins with death, not life.

## EPILOGUE: LEADING WITH DEPRESSION & ANXIETY

Depression and anxiety have been in my life for a long time, and my career as a pastor has been one in which I've had to learn to deal with, and work alongside, both. So in a kind of follow-up to my story above, I want to let you in on several practices I keep sacred. Perhaps these may be of help to you.

### TRANSPARENCY

Being upfront with my congregation about the breakage in my life has done a lot for me (and I suppose for them, too), not least the assurance that I don't need to steal away and hide behind some made-up story of a life of togetherness. It's best to be an honest leader. My congregation knows that I've been to counseling. It knows that I take medication. It knows that worry can follow me around. It knows that I can disappear in certain situations. While I recognize this sort of thing could be a potential occupational hazard for some of you, I really hope you have people in your congregation who will allow you to unravel in front of them, and who will walk with you in your honesty and openness.

## AWARENESS

It's been good for me to know (and almost make a list of) various scenarios and experiences that often impose extra stress into my life. This is not so that I may avoid them when they come. That's not very helpful. It's so that I may be conscious of what it is that may be causing me to feel certain things (often negative) about myself. Sit down and make a list of particular conversations or leadership situations or pastoral offices that cause stress and anxiety for you. Then build scripts to get through those, and reactions you may try in the future. Better yet, have your closest co-leaders (staff, elders, etc.) make the list for you. Trust me...they already know!

## SUPPORT

Our church funds the value of counseling. When a member of our church desires to go, we help pay the bill if needed. It's also a "perk" of being on my staff. Everyone has that at their disposal. Sitting down with someone who is an expert on mental and emotional dynamics has, at times, been a necessary thing for me. Sometimes they say, "You're fine. Let it go." Other times they say, "Let's do some work on this." Find a counseling center nearby, and build that bridge.

I'm sure you already know this, but leadership doesn't fix internal weakness. It irritates it. It draws it out. And simply "holding it together" in order to come across tidy and stable won't do. Self-deception flows away from community, and the distance will only increase. It doesn't work. And as my wife says: "Crazy don't hide for too long." Do what you can to stay healthy! And email me if you need to.

- ON THE ROPES -

# KNOCKED DOWN, BUT NOT OUT

*by Chad Simpkins*

I hate losing. It is not something I find enjoyable. I am VERY competitive. In fact, when I was in college, my intramural basketball team was really good. We knew we were good. Everyone told us we were good. We were the overwhelming choice to win the intramural league championship. If Vegas had odds on our tournament, we would have been the hands down favorite. Just hand us the trophy!

Something strange happened in the semifinals. We lost. We didn't lose to just any team. We didn't lose to a team with better players than we had. We lost to a team made up of soccer players! The ultimate insult.

I was mad. Angry. Livid. I needed to release the pent up steam inside! Our 'bench' for the game consisted of a neat row of folding chairs. I proceeded to use one of those chairs as a soccer ball and kicked it across the basketball floor (ala Bobby Knight). Interesting the distance a chair goes when kicked. To this day, my wife retells this story to our kids and they make fun of me. Which they should.

Losing. Is. Not. Fun. Thankfully, as I age, I handle losing with much more grace. Chairs appreciate that.

In September 2009, my wife and I made a decision which culminated in fulfilling a dream of ours eight years in the making. Our family would be moving to Chapel Hill, NC, to plant a brand new church. Friends told us we were going to plant a great church. Family told us we were going to plant a great church. People in our church planting circles told us we were going to plant a great church. We BELIEVED we were going to plant a great church. My competitive nature would settle for nothing less.

It was January 2010. I resigned from my campus pastor position at a wonderful church outside of DC, in Virginia. Due to the time spent there with the staff and leaders, we felt prepared for our next steps to plant. I spent a few weeks training my replacement whom I could tell was going to be a strong leader. Everything setup perfectly for our transition. Two weeks prior to moving, I attended a church planting bootcamp in Johnson City, Tennessee. I spent the week learning the nuts and bolts of church planting while working on details for our new church.

The end of the week approached. My mind overflowed with information (I am pretty sure I bled information from my ears). Two of the main contributors to our church planting network were in attendance. We sat down to talk about the start-up capital for our church plant. I thought I knew where things were for us financially. Apparently, not.

One of the representatives in the meeting led a local church in the Triangle. They were the reason we were moving to Chapel Hill. I was excited to work with them, to learn from them, to be supported by them.

In our meeting that morning, we listed all of our network partners and the amount of money they were going to give to our project. Our supporting local church's name came up; "So, you guys are in for $50,000, correct?" It really wasn't even a question. It was more of a statement knowing the answer - so we thought. The pastor looked at me and replied, "I know we said we could give you $50,000, but we can't. In fact, we can't give you any money."

Pregnant pause.

I laughed.

What else could I do in the moment? No amount of yelling, screaming, throwing notebooks, kicking chairs was going to change anything.

So I just laughed.

This church recruited us to plant our church. They were the reason we chose Chapel Hill. I couldn't go back to my old job. We were taking our oldest child out of her current school the next week. We had already rented a townhouse in Chapel Hill. New renters waited to move into our home in Virginia. We sat in the no-turning-back moment...and I laughed. What else could I do?

Needless to say, the drive back home wasn't as fun as the drive to Tennessee. I drove back to northern Virginia confused by what had happened. I wondered what it all meant. What would we do now? How would this change things? I mean, could anything else bad happen?

Yes.

About 45 minutes from home, I see smoke billowing behind my car. I thought, "Wow, what is going on behind me? Something must be wrong with somebody's car." Then I looked at my dashboard. That somebody was me. My car's temperature gauge pegged beyond HOT - I was pretty sure it was stuck on HELL. I slowed down and pulled off the road as smoke shot out of my hood. Seems my car's water pump blew. Could someone give me a chair to kick? I mean, it couldn't get worse could it?

Still reeling from the meeting and car repairs, we pressed on. That next Saturday, the weekend of our move, my family piled in our minivan and headed 45 minutes away to pick up our U-Haul for the move to North Carolina. Our plan for the day was a quick turn around. Get in, grab the

U-Haul, get out and head home to start loading. There was a slight problem. The truck we ordered wasn't there yet. It was SUPPOSED to be there for us but it wasn't. So we sat. And waited. Time ticked, ticked, ticked away. After a couple of hours - HOURS - our truck came in! We were ready to head home and a tad upset.

It started snowing.

We had a long way to go to get home and the snow falling wasn't flurries. It was coming down hard. Real hard. Driving a 26-foot long U-Haul in the blowing snow isn't my idea of fun. Thankfully, we finally made it home. The trip took almost two hours. Everything would fall into place now.

Another problem arose. The next day, many people from the church we were leaving were coming to help us load the truck. The aforementioned snow turned into a snowstorm that night. The next morning, we woke up to close to a foot and a half of snow.

What a perfect few weeks this was turning out to be. The snow was deep, the roads were bad, no one would show.

However, people trickled in. Many of them. They helped pack our truck. They fed us pizza. They encouraged us. They shed tears with us. They wished us well. "You'll plant a great church!" they said as they waved goodbye. Maybe this church plant thing WAS going to be great?!

I sit here, six years later, at a booth in Dunkin Donuts, just outside Duke University. This Dunkin Donuts may have the worst wi-fi in the world. I am partly here for the wifi, but mostly to drink my favorite cup of coffee. As I sit here, I can honestly tell you I feel wounded, bleeding, wondering about the church we planted. What happened? What happened to that big, great church we were supposed to plant? What happened to the success so many believed would come? Why did I not feel successful?

I am mostly an extrovert, but have some introverted tendencies. I enjoy being around people. I energize from those interactions. Yet, I find I struggle being around other pastors. It's not that I don't like pastors, I grew up a PK (not a Place Kicker but a Preacher's Kid). I am comfortable in the world of pastors. I struggle being around them because of how I view the church we planted. I do not feel successful.

In the pastoral world, we ask questions adopted from American corporate success: it's all about the numbers. We ask number questions: How many are you averaging? How much do people give each week? Don't get me wrong, I like knowing how others are doing. I DESIRE for other pastors churches to grow! However, I hate telling how WE are doing. I measured my success based on the numbers AND based on comparing our church to others.

When I begin to compare my expectations with our reality, I get this overwhelming feeling I am a failure. I also feel I let many people down. I let our supporters down, my family down, myself down. Even the people in the church we planted, I feel I let them down. My competitive nature gets the best of me in these moments.

It would be one thing if we never tried to grow our church. We've tried. We held large events, sent out the postcards, watched as many showed up for community projects, we attempted everything possible. No matter what we tried, momentum never came and stayed. Momentum liked to come over to the house, have a slice of pizza, then leave a few minutes later. It showed up for three or four weeks, then POOF! Gone. I wish I could marry Momentum; that way she would stay at our house. Apparently, she has commitment issues.

I played over and over in my mind the scenarios of how someone else or something else may have caused us to be 'unsuccessful.' We didn't get that $50,000. We didn't get enough local support from area churches. We planted in a very unchurched community. Granted, all of these could be small reasons for our current situation but they weren't the problem. I figured out the problem.

The problem was me.

I defined my success by what I didn't have, or how I compared to others, or by what I thought went 'wrong.' In reality, something was missing. Something big. Something real. Something true.

I was missing everything that had gone right. I was missing Jesus at work in our story the whole time! Over the last few months, I started taking inventory of what Jesus was doing while I was worrying about success. Here are a few items I came up with...

We baptized 24 people in five years. In some churches, that happens in one day. It took us five years (again, number comparisons). Then I look at those who took that step of faith: teenagers, UNC students, two of my children, young adults, couples, an 84 year old grandmother, families, and Paul.

Paul ended up in a wheelchair from a car accident. He started attending from day one. We baptized Paul. When we baptized him, it took five men to do it. Paul's a tall guy and due to his rigid body from the accident, we couldn't sit him in the horse trough like everyone else. We had to dip him into the water starting from his head and making our way down to his feet. I'll never forget that.

When we launched the church, we decided through a 'Community Needs Assessment' we would focus on food insecurity for children. We started out handing out boxes of food to under resourced families. Then we began gathering canned goods for local backpack programs. Next, we worked with our school system to hand out lunches during the summer to kids who were out of school. Last summer, through this program, we handed out over 3000 lunches to under resourced children in our community. I keep meeting people in town who tell me, "Everyone in the community says your church is doing more for child hunger than anyone else here." We have a rep for helping kids who need food. This year, our new mayor made child hunger a priority. The first time we met, she told me we were on the top of her list to lead this summer's initiative with the town's backing. Our church is at the head of the table leading our town through this program to feed 1500 kids a lunch every day this summer.

I sat and watched marriages heal; marriages at the end of their rope. A conversation, a message, or a small group gave them what they needed to try one more time. Now those marriages are thriving.

Two mother-in-laws (one who attends our church, one who does not), tell me all the time how our church changed their lives. One's son and the other's daughter started attending when we launched. These two young people met. They went out on a date. Then a few more dates. I ended up marrying the couple. They are good friends of our family.. Now they are expecting their first child. And those mother-in-laws are going to be grandparents.


We have people who at one point in time were integral parts of our church. They moved away or moved on. Yet, they still give. I tell them they can stop giving. They remind me of the impact the church had on their lives and how they want to continue to help impacting Chapel Hill. So they keep on giving to help transform more lives.

Then there is the family who lives on Long Island. I have never met them. If they walked into our church tomorrow, I would not know them. They heard about our church plant before we started. They started giving to our church. They continue to give to our church. They even bless our family financially throughout the year, which allows us to take some vacation time. I don't know if we'll ever meet them. No matter what, they bless our church and continue to give.

I can easily get stuck, upset that my expectations for our church are not being met. I try to define success the way the world defines success. That reality can feel like a weight shackled to my ankles. It can consume me. Yet when I sit back and really look at the picture that has unfolded, I see God has had His hand in this from the start. Lives have been changed. Lives are being changed. Lives will continue to be changed. The truth is, we DID plant a great church with great people doing great things!

Slowly, I am getting to a place of understanding that it isn't my definition of success that matters. It's what God is up to that matters. Success is a burden I place on myself. I am still trying. I am still learning. I still hold onto hope we will grow in every way possible. But now I can let God be the writer of our 'success.'

An interesting addendum to this story: back to that $50,000. Remember the church who couldn't help us? The church who bailed on us one week before we moved? The pastor and I got together a couple of years ago and talked. He explained to me what was going on at the time and why the decision had been made. I fully understood. I harbor no ill will. We are friends. And later on this year, we will become a campus of that church.

God has a weird sense of humor.

- ON THE ROPES -

# I WAS TRAINED FOR THIS

*by Marques Evans*

*Life will try to knock your lights out*
*Like a gang of infidels with the pipes out*
*Taking blows, trying to send me where my soul goes*
*But I oppose, strategies from my souls foe*

That is a line from a rap song I performed back in 2010 with a couple of brothers from the Revolution 216, the church I planted in Cleveland, Ohio. This verse relates to being up against the ropes. It seems I have been up against the ropes my whole life.

From the melanin in my skin,
to the side of town I was born on,
to the ghetto where I was raised,
to the poverty I experienced,

to overcoming sickness as a child,

to the times I fought to make the grades so I could continue to play
   high school basketball at the private Catholic school I attended,

to barely graduating,

to surviving suburban Cleveland,

to the junior college I attended for two very hard years,

to the gangs and drugs which were so pervasive in my neighborhood I
   didn't think I would live to the age of 20,

to the police harassment I experienced too many times to even count,
   and yet I am still here.

I was trained for this.

The problem I see with today's church planting organizations is that
they look for people who seem to have it all together: perfect families,
perfect grades, perfect credit scores, flawless launch plans, perfect looks, and
perfect connections with the right demographics. When you are in the
middle of the streets where life happens, and you plant a church
community, perfection goes out the window.

The church I attended growing up was in a rough neighborhood, but I
grew up in a religious home. My mother basically was a single parent who
raised four boys. We survived on government assistance while she attended
community college to become a registered nurse. She did it! She raised us
during the crack era. My father succumbed to the drug and struggled to
overcome its power. Thankfully, he beat it. Due to his struggle, my parents
divorced - twice.

You see, I was trained for this.

I've seen and lived through struggle. I've experienced, on numerous
occasions, being misunderstood, ridiculed and judged based on my height,
economic status and of course, the color of my skin. I am not the least bit
afraid of rejection. I've learned fear can be a blessing and a curse.

I've watched as two of my brothers worked to pay their way through
college. I've had a ringside seat as my youngest brother fought through

physical and financial hardships. All of them did this in their late 20's. We were trained for this.

Paul tells us in 1 Corinthians 9:27 (NLT)...

## I DISCIPLINE MY BODY LIKE AN ATHLETE, TRAINING IT TO DO WHAT IT SHOULD. OTHERWISE, I FEAR THAT AFTER PREACHING TO OTHERS I MYSELF MIGHT BE DISQUALIFIED.

Maybe you have a sport you enjoy. However, because you enjoy that sport it doesn't mean you have what it takes to succeed in that sport. For instance, you might be a die-hard boxing fan. You may be able to regurgitate every stat, of every champ, in every weight class. But do you really know what it takes to be a boxer? Have you ever laced up the gloves? Gone through the rigorous training that goes into being a boxer? Perfected your jab? Learned how to counter punch? Worked on conditioning and strengthening your core? Ever spent time working on speed with sprints and jump roping? If you have never been hit, then how will you fare against a hungry, seasoned fighter whose intent is to obliterate you? Will you be able to deal with being on the ropes, taking the hardest punches of your life?

In life, there exists an adversary who wants to win at all costs. This 'opponent' has been taking good people, like you and me, out for thousands of years. One by one, this fighter's opponents experienced the ropes and the eventual knockouts. Anyone who underestimated the lengths this enemy would go to found themselves knocked out, cold. This enemy has a purpose: to destroy the image and will of the Most High and anyone else who steps into this ring. Do we fully understand the nature of the enemy we face as church planters and people?

The scriptures make it clear in John 10:10 (GNT)...

## THE THIEF COMES ONLY IN ORDER TO STEAL, KILL, AND DESTROY. I HAVE COME IN ORDER THAT YOU MIGHT HAVE LIFE - LIFE IN ALL ITS FULLNESS.

Satan, our opponent, is a thief. He will kill and he wants to destroy our lives. The words John writes must be clear to us when we are making the decision to step into this life or death situation called ministry. John's words are an amazing reminder of the power of Jesus over Satan. They are words of wisdom for us, our families and also for the people we are trying to reach. It's imperative that we make our calling and election sure. A tough opponent awaits in the ring.

In the five years of leading our community, Revolution 216, we found ourselves against the ropes many times. Countless incidents where we were in situations that could have gone bad real quick. I mean life-lost bad. I'm talking not-coming-back bad. Guns about-to-be-pulled bad. It's interesting how our contexts can be so different.

One day, I sat listening to a church leader complain about how people were talking about him and the difficulty he felt in how to deal with the gossip. I honestly believe he felt hurt by the things said about him. I would never disregard his feelings outwardly, but in my mind I was thinking, are you serious? The worries I carry every day are a lot bigger than a few words. I worry about people being robbed, shot, or killed. I'm more worried about people going to jail. I worry that a friendly protest, infused with the right ingredients, could turn into a racially motivated riot. I worry about innocent children being killed in the places where my children live and play. I worry about the people in my community with no hope, who give up and commit suicide. I worry that people I know may not have enough money for food or rent. I'm more worried about sharing the Gospel with drug dealers and the police pulling up and arresting everybody on the scene, including me, because I look like the people I am so desperately trying to reach. In the end, I could care less about what somebody in a church thinks or says about me. This is the context I live and serve in.

I was trained for this.

"You have to understand; the harder the practice, the easier the game."

Those words are mine. They help me get through every day. They remind me of a prominent figure in the original covenant about Moses. Moses ran from the luxury of Pharaoh's palace and the privileges which accompanied it. God trained him in the desert and wilderness before he was called by The Most High to deliver the people of Israel out of the bondage of Egyptian slavery. Moses learned the ways of a shepherd. He began to understand the tendencies of the sheep. He was deprogrammed from the conditioning of Egypt. He experienced firsthand the power of The Most High and saw God eliminate the excuses he carried around. He experienced firsthand the wilderness he and the people of Israel would have to wander through in order to possess the land of Canaan. Trust built in The Most High allowed Moses to stand in front of Pharaoh and declare the emancipation of a whole nation of people. Moses then had to convince these people that he was the real deal.

He was trained for his mission.

Do you remember the story? Moses' back was against the ropes many times in his life: when he fought with Pharaoh, when they faced the potential end at the Red Sea, when the Israelites complained - about everything, when the people rebelled and created a golden calf to worship, when a whole generation of people died in the wilderness. To top it off, after forty years of wandering and Moses still never set foot inside the Promise Land.

Are you prepared for this fight? Are you trained enough that you would willingly give your own blood, sweat and tears? Are you ready to lose friendships because you believe in the mission God sent you on? Do you think you can handle the blows of misunderstandings you will face with your team? Not to mention the tension you will experience with your family? Are you prepared that you may never see your vision come to fruition, but that the next generation may see it through? This is the most important fight in the world and it may cost you everything.

If you are in this fight because you think it's sexy, or someone with charisma convinced you to lace up, you might want to get out now. In this ring, you and your family are going to directly take the blows of the enemy. Please hear me - it hurts. You must be confident in your decision to step into the ring. You must have the resolve that compares to the willpower of Evander Holyfield, Roberto Duran, Sugar Ray Leonard, Manny Pacquiao, Muhammad Ali, Oscar Dela Hoya, Mike Tyson and a host of other great fighters who all understood they would eventually find themselves against the ropes. Of course, our fight is different than what these men faced. It's harder, cuts deeper, hurts worse, heals slower, but its impact is eternal.

Scripture says in 1 Peter 4:12 (KJV)...

## BELOVED, THINK IT NOT STRANGE CONCERNING THE FIERY TRIAL WHICH IS TO TRY YOU, AS THOUGH SOME STRANGE THING HAPPENED UNTO YOU...

If you are thinking of planting a community of faith, if you are sure about your call to plant a church, then my friend, you better make sure you were trained for this. When you are against the ropes, your training is all you have. Through prayer, study and a willingness to trust the Word of our Heavenly Father, through the power of His Spirit, I have personally bounced back off the ropes many times. I give God the praise through his Son, through whom salvation is received. His sovereignty has been training you for such a time as this. Now, let's get in the ring and fight!

# DO THE RIGHT THING AND GET PUMMELED FOR IT!

*by Chris Stoval*

My wife and I planted a church in the northern suburbs of Atlanta. The excitement surrounding this church was very high. We were planting the church in an emerging area. The technology boom was occurring here and people in droves were moving in.

Our desire for the church was to be very edgy. This was on purpose. In this way, we could specialize in reaching the unchurched, dechurched and spiritually disenfranchised. The atmosphere we created was a mix between a restaurant/bar and a church. Everyone sat at round tables and greeters/ushers operated more like waiters and waitresses. This method worked! In the first seven years, the church exploded with growth. Every year we grew. By 2007, we were regularly running over 400 people for weekend services.

Around 2006, my most integral staff member left. He was recently engaged and his wife-to-be's work would take them to Florida. I hated to see him go. Together, we had essentially planted the church. Our partnership went all the way back to when we were meeting as a small house church. Even though I was very happy for him, his departure had an affect on our church - and our attendance.

Despite a tough transition of seeing him leave, we moved forward and brought a new staff member onboard. This staff member was confident, energetic and talented which made the transition much easier. After a year with the new staff member, everything looked good. Our attendance was holding solid and we seemed to be moving forward.

And then it happened.

On two different occasions other people on staff came to me with concerns about our newest staff person. I took their concerns seriously and started looking into what had been brought to my attention. We found out our newest staff member - who was married with two kids - was having extramarital affairs with two married women in our church. I never saw this coming. It was like it dropped out of the sky and that sky was very dark.

I informed our elders and we agreed on a plan that would be full of grace. Too often I have watched churches get in situations like this and prioritize protecting themselves over restoring someone. With a plan full of grace ready to go, one of our elders and I went to this staff member and confronted him about this sin. We offered the resources of the church to do whatever would be necessary to restore his marriage. We went a step further to say that we believed in grace and we wanted God to have a great victory here. We offered to keep his job waiting for him so we could hopefully see him fully restored into ministry. He denied he was having an extramarital affair. He refused the grace and renewal laid out before him. At that point, there was no other choice but to dismiss him. We all agreed to keep everything confidential, legally appropriate and to part ways. As tough as this experience was, we felt we were full of grace and did the right thing.

A few days after our meeting, my phone started blowing up. Word trickled out and we were in the middle of a disaster. I called an emergency meeting of the elders to discuss the situation. No one had broken confidence to anyone in the church or even to their spouses. Then we learned where the leak came from. The staff member we recently let go had begun contacting church members and revealing what we had accused him of and more. He was telling the people in our church that because he was a minority, we let him go out of racism. The rumors being circulated also accused the church leadership of terminating him because we were intimidated by his spiritual maturity and influence. He also told people we were not a Biblical church, nor a Biblical leadership, and our attempt to defame him was evidence of this. He also informed people he contacted he would be starting his own church. Not only should members leave our church, but that they were welcomed to attend his new work.

In one week, our attendance dropped from over 400 to less than 100. Initially, around 100 people went to this former staff member's church. The rest just went away. Many of the people we were reaching came to us with dysfunctional feelings about church. This episode only confirmed their doubts. I believe to this day many have never darkened the door of a church again. About six months later, that same staff member was caught in his sin and both affairs were revealed. Eventually, all three families were ripped apart. A few months later, the spouse of the ex-staff member came to us and asked forgiveness for the things she had said when the accusations were made. She had stood by her husband and held firm to her beliefs that her husband was innocent and wrongly accused. I always held her in high regard and her humility to take this step of reconciliation only increased my regard for her.

We pulled up our bootstraps and attempted to pick ourselves up to bring the church back together. The church was doing well and over the next few months we were able to get our attendance back above 150. We seemed poised to grow above 200.

And then the stock market crash of 2008 hit.

When we planted the church, we strategically located the church in what was called the "Silicon Valley of the South." Nortel Networks had their headquarters here as well as several other '.com' companies. Once the market crashed, any attendance increase we regained immediately was cut in half. Many of our people were devastated financially. They moved in with family in other areas of the country. Some went back to California. Others left our church for larger more established churches believing they needed a church where they could network with more people. Some felt they needed a church who had better bandwidth to take care of them if things got really desperate.

Our attendance dropped to below 50 people.

Let me give you an idea of where we were as a church at this point. We were in a building with a $2.5 million mortgage - and 50 people. You don't have to be a math wizard to figure this out...we were in the hole, big time! Prior to the economic crash, our building was worth $3.2 million. In order to be responsible to our lender we placed the building up for sale. We couldn't even get an offer of $1 million. What made things worse was for me was that when we moved into this building, I wanted to lease and everyone convinced me that buying was the only way to go. As you can imagine, most of our staff left. Those who didn't leave became part-time staff. We couldn't afford to pay anyone. We also owed a personal friend of mine $80,000 for a complete HVAC replacement for a building I didn't want to own in the first place and we had no way to pay this back.

At this point I was ready to wave the white flag and quit. But the people that were still with us wanted to try and save it. The confirmation to hang in there came from the president of the company holding our building's mortgage, who was also a dear friend. He called me out of the blue and said, "Do you remember the parable of the King who forgave the debt? Go and take what's left of your church and see if you can save it. We're eating this building either way, so let's try and not let a church die as well."

I felt God was in this. Being a "take the hill" kind of guy, I imagined the great testimony we could tell of how horrifically bad everything was and how God brought victory as this church grew and prospered. We found a church with a chapel they weren't using and they agreed to lease the space to us. The pastor agreed to halve the rent the first three months in order to help us out. God was moving and this was exciting. We set everything into motion and launched our Sunday service in our new location. The church was doing well and seemed to be healing from all we experienced. There were a few upgrades which needed to be done to the facility, so with some meager fundraising efforts we were able to make improvements to the building. We understood the building wasn't ours but we felt - based on the generosity of this other church - this was a way we could repay them and do the right thing.

During our first year in the space, we started to grow a little despite everything we had been through. One day, the new executive pastor of the church we were leasing from called me. He explained their Finance Team met and they were increasing our rent by 80%. He further explained we had 30 days to decide if we were going to pay the rent or not. Initially, when we rented the facility we wanted a written lease. The pastor insisted as Christians we should be able to trust each other and refused to sign a lease. They were raising our rent 80% and we had no recourse. We had just gotten to the point where we were becoming healthy spiritually and financially. Money set aside for marketing and outreach would now go to rent. I knew this was a sign the church wanted us out of there. The problem? We had no where to go. We ended up agreeing to the rent increase and believed God would provide.

In year two, we were surviving. Without any resources to reach out into the community and let them know we existed, it was almost impossible to get new people to show up. However, we kept plugging along. Then the executive pastor from the church we were renting from showed up again. I was ready for him to tell us the rent was increasing. Instead, he informed me we had three months to move out. I asked if there was anything we could do to stay. He informed me that a private school was willing to pay more and we need to go.

We had three months to figure out where we were going. Our leadership started looking everywhere and the only option we could come up with was a school. A good friend of mine was a local principal and he agreed to lease us space on Sundays. At this point, the problem we faced was being a beaten-down, older church trying to go back to being a portable church. This meant set-up and teardown. Something we had moved away from a few years earlier. For the next few months we held our own, but more people left simply because they weren't interested in doing set-up and teardown again.

We now knew it was time to shut it down. We made sure everyone who stuck around found a church to attend. Then we laid her to rest with our final service. And that was it...I was finished.

I think back about our church now and realize maybe God wanted me to shut things down years earlier but I missed it. The reason I missed it is because quitting is not in my DNA. To say I was not mad at God would be a lie. I felt completely rejected by God. I felt like I didn't matter to God. I was bitter because I went out of my way to try and do everything the right way. Through every situation being full of grace. Yet, as I looked back at the church, what were the results? The church we worked so hard to build was no more. Here I stood, feeling like I was holding the bag of all the terrible decisions that had been made. I trusted with an absolute faith God was going to make all this work out...but it didn't.

I fell into a deep depression full of resentment. I resented people who were part of the church plant. I resented people whom I had ministered to and stood by. I felt like they had not stood by me. We were generous and patient with so many people but when things got tough, they got up and left. There were those who said they would stand by us until the bitter end. Yet, they left and never came back, without even talking to us. Others needed to salve their conscience for leaving and made up stories to justify their lack of loyalty to our church. My heart was broken.

Closing our church was right up there with the death of both of my parents. I can remember waking up that first Monday morning after we closed the church. I struggled because for the first time in 25 years I did not have a church to lead. Why didn't I have a church to lead? Was it because of moral failure on my part? No, I worked very hard to run away from even the slightest temptation in this area. Was it because of a lack of commitment? No, I worked myself until I couldn't work anymore. I walked on faith that would have shaken seasoned Christians.

No church to lead and to top it off, my wife Susy and I were broke. We found ourselves with significant unsecured debt. We personally financed many aspects of the church during those final years. When the stock market initially crashed, I didn't take a salary for an entire year. I felt it would help our church pull together financially. It didn't help. I even started other businesses in order to provide for my family so I could still serve as pastor of the church. Why would God not honor my faithfulness and loyalty? Why doesn't God like me?

During this time, I met up with one very loyal friend who stood by me through all of this. One day he asked me how I was doing. There weren't words that could describe the pain. I told him I was very frustrated and confused about God and my existence in ministry. The metaphor I painted was of a room filled with all the pastors in the country. On the front row were all of God's "golden boys" - names you would be familiar with. The next few rows were filled with pastors God was blessing. I wasn't seated in any of those rows. I would ask God, "Why won't You bless me? I can preach as well as most of these guys; I'm more committed to the work of the local church than most of these guys; I'm a student of leadership and lead as well as any of these guys. In fact, most of these other pastors would have quit and/or run if You had put them through what I have had to go through." I felt as if God was pointing a finger at me and saying, "Be quiet! You're lucky I even let you in the room in the first place!"

After some awkward and quiet moments, my friend responded. "I think I see why all of this has happened to you. Could I share with you?" I answered, "Please!"

He began to explain, "I don't think your metaphor and description of the room is at all correct. I think the metaphor is that of a General. Sometimes there are missions that are very important, but they are not the least appealing. The General would like to send someone more expendable, but the problem is the mission is so tough and so unappealing that the soldier would either quit or be killed before he completed the mission. This particular mission is very important. The General is reluctantly going to have to send a soldier who could easily do a myriad of other missions with great success. The single reason why the General is going to have to use a solider like this is because this soldier won't quit! No matter how insignificant the mission seems, or how difficult it gets, this soldier will attack it as if the world depends on the mission's success. This soldier will not quit no matter what. Chris, you're that kind of soldier. No matter what God gave you, you wouldn't lay down and die…you wouldn't quit. The reason you wouldn't quit is simply because God asked you to do it."

I can't tell you the flood of emotions I felt at that moment. Even now as I write these words I feel that same feeling. My friend's words were a balm on my broken heart. God spoke through him to help me understand this hellish path. He helped me understand I had been selected for ministry special ops. I felt incredible gratitude for his words.

If you are reading this story and have been broken and hurt by ministry, remember, you have been chosen for ministry special ops. It is an honor to have you read my words and it is an honor to serve with you. I hope God would use my words to bring you some level of healing and purpose, just as my friend's words were a balm for me.

## - ON THE ROPES -

# BLOODIED, BRUISED AND BEAT UP

*by Trevor DeVage*

The first punch was a haymaker. I didn't even see it coming. I stumbled and got weak in the knees. I simply fell backwards hoping the ropes were close enough to keep me on my feet. After being in the fight for fourteen years prior, I had never had my proverbial bell rung like that before. You may be thinking, "You boxed for fourteen years?" Well not exactly. However, going into my first lead pastor position, I had been in ministry for fourteen years. Sometimes that feels like you have been in the ring for fourteen years.

On the night in question, where I felt wind leave my lungs, it was these words that rocked me to the core and thrust me against the ropes, *"You are the worst leader I have ever encountered. Mark my words, this church will have a for sale sign in front of it in less than a year."*

Now don't get me wrong, I do not think that I am the greatest leader on the planet. I do however think God has given me gifts to lead a church. I had been leading in a healthy and fast growing church the ten years prior to taking on this lead pastor position. Yet that was the first of many blows that night. My character was hit with an uppercut. My integrity took a body blow. My leadership took repeated jabs to the face and stomach.

I remember sitting in the room that night taking blow after blow. For two and a half hours I listened. I didn't fight back, I simply took the punches. I was bouncing off the ropes of life with every other sentence uttered. I began to question whether or not I should just fall to the floor and allow myself to be counted out. I wondered if I should just throw my hands in the air, give up and get out of the ring. In my fourteen years of ministry, I had never been in such a battle. I had never been this wounded, bloodied, and bruised.

What took me by surprise the most was that this was coming from the chairman of the elders. This was the man that had pursued me, wooed me, cared for me, and believed in me. He told me the good, the bad, and the ugly of the church I was going to lead. He used phrases like, "We have to bust up the country club." He painted a vision of a church that was ready to move forward with vigor and grit. He told me that he longed for a church that would reach deeper into our community. He drove down how he saw us reaching people that were far from God. Not only that, he treated me like a son.

When he was landing blow after blow to my heart and soul, it literally felt like my father had turned his fists on me. I was in a haze and life seemed to slow down and ministry was becoming fuzzy. It was like a Rocky movie where Balboa gets hit over and over and the camera makes it look like nothing is in focus.

Twelve weeks earlier I had moved my family across the country to hopefully start what would be the last ministry we would ever have to interview at. Now, I didn't know if I would even make it to the six month mark. In those twelve weeks we had seen close to a thousand new people come through our doors. We had baptized 29 people on one weekend. We had the largest Easter to date in our church. How on earth did we get from that, just a few weeks prior, to this?

How did we go from praying, laughing, hugging, and supporting each other, to backbiting, name calling, and haymakers? It is one of the things that hurts my heart most about the church sometimes. We are willing to try and knock one another out before we are willing to help each other off the mat. I expect it to come from the outside world. I expect it to come from the enemy. I didn't expect it to come from my corner man. This was the guy who was supposed to be encouraging me in the midst of the fight. This was the man who was supposed to be cleaning up my wounds. It turned out this was the guy who actually sucker punched me into the ropes.

The meeting that night lasted four long hours. Things eventually calmed down - we even embraced - but we knew it was going to be work to get through this. Four weeks later he resigned as chairman and left the church. I was devastated.

For the next six months to a year there was not a day that went by where I did not want to quit and simply fall to the mat for a ten count. However, God did not allow that to happen. As a matter of fact, He did the opposite. He began to surround me with godly men that were willing to actually be my corner guys.

These men came from everywhere. Some were other elders that were in the room that night. They surrounded me, cleaned the blood off of my soul, and spurred me back into the ring. Some were pastors and leaders from around the country that somehow made their way into my life at "just the right time" to speak words of affirmation, love, and to encourage me. Some were men in my church who felt as if I needed a few guys that would allow me to simply be me. They gave me a safe place to figure out what was next.

There was one phrase that all of these different men spoke into my life over and over. At one point, I thought they had all somehow secretly gotten to know each other and agreed to say the same words to me. Those words were simply this, "STAY THE COURSE." Those three little words kept creeping into my life through all of the people I mentioned above. There were days that I didn't want to stay the course and inevitably those were the days someone would call and say to me, "Hey man...just stay the course. You are going to be fine." As much as I did not want to hear that, they were right. As long I stayed on the ropes for a few brief moments and caught my breath I would be fine. Eventually, the bell was going to ring and the round would be over.

Sometimes when the fists are flying and you're bouncing off the ropes, all you can do is put your hands over your face and wait for the bell. That's the funny thing about ministry; there is always a bell that ends a round and a bell that leads to a new round. There is always a corner to go to, a stool to sit on, words of encouragement, and the opportunity to get back up and into the fight.

Some of the greatest fights I have ever watched were the ones where the fight seemed to be over. During the previous round, there had been an "on the ropes" battle; the end looked to be coming soon. However, the fighter who looked defeated the round before came back only to knock their opponent out. The beautiful thing about following Christ is that we have already won the battle that is worth fighting. We have already been assured that we get the heavyweight title because our fight has already been fought. Our real opponent has been defeated. The problem is that we forget that the real enemy is not the elder, the church member, the critic, or the staff member. The real enemy is not the person across the aisle from us on a Sunday morning. Our real enemy is the one that scripture says, "prowls around like a roaring lion waiting to devour. " I guess it makes sense for Satan to attack from where we would expect support. If our enemy can convince our corner men to jump into the ring and get us on the ropes for him, he can sit back and just watch.

The bell eventually rang. I was able to go to my corner, get some rest and hear words of encouragement. I felt beat up and bloodied, but I was not out of the fight. For the better part of six months I sat in the corner healing and resting. There were numerous men that surrounded me and put salve on my wounds. They iced the swelling under my eyes. My vision for our church started to become clearer and clearer. I found myself up against the ropes, but made it to the bell. I was willing to get back in the ring for another round and God has done some pretty unreal things since then.

During the last three years, we have seen significant kingdom growth at our church. Marriages have been restored, families renewed, and lives redeemed in ways we could have never imagined. It all started with a conscious decision to not fall to the mat, but to stay up on the ropes, take the blows, and make it to the bell. We are far from done, but I have a feeling that if we stay the course and remember that we already have the heavyweight champion belt in our possession, we may just come back and win the match with a knockout of our own.

Today, if you feel as if you are barely standing and your back is against the ropes remember these words...STAY THE COURSE. When you survive blood, bruises, and body blows, you are prepared to help those that have been on the ropes of life too.

# STANDING

### EIGHT COUNT

— ROUND THREE —

## - STANDING EIGHT COUNT -

# A TERRIBLE SAVIOR

*by Dave Milam*

Most Pastors eventually reach a moment when they second guess their calling and dream of flipping burgers. "It would be easier," we suppose. I hit that wall after seven years of church planting. Burnout had set in and the weight of ministry was beginning to wreck my soul.

About an hour north of New Orleans sat a small plantation on the bayou where I would spend the first five days of my ten week sabbatical. Dr. Eddie Parish owned the place.

He was a tall, lanky man with a grey, hippie ponytail and goatee. Hardly what I expected for a therapist. If I didn't know better, I'd have guessed he had a lead pipe behind his back and was hankering to bust some kneecaps. He wore a grey t-shirt tucked into a pair of coffee brown cargo shorts. The slight bounce in his gait revealed he was comfortable in his skin.

There was no lead pipe, so I extended my hand and said hello. Eddie leaned in, sidestepping my hand along with every social boundary, to give me a fierce bear hug with complete indifference to my personal space. I think he was happy to see me. He was strong. His grip squeezed the air out of my lungs and lasted long enough to be awkward. Then, he let go and introduced himself. I guess that's how they do it in the bayou.

As we sat down, I began my prepared presentation on, 'How he would help me,' with ten bullet points listed in order of priority. I had also taken the liberty of graphing my burnout over time, along with a flow chart containing possible causes. As an appendix, I included a bibliography of burnout self-help books I planned to read while I was there. I was ready to go.

I finished my presentation. He sat silent and stared. This was not good. Perhaps I had missed something on my list that would be critical to my recovery. What could it be? I wondered.

Finally he spoke, "Man. You need to slow down."

"I know! That's bullet point number 3: 'Slow down.'" I pointed to my list while agreeing.

His hand reached for my journal and began stacking my books together. He looked me in the eyes and said slowly, "Here's what I want you to do. No more reading. No writing or trying to figure anything out. And for goodness sake, turn off your cell phone. For the next four hours, I want you to simply 'be.'"

Confused and panicked, I pleaded, "Okay, but I thought we were going to fix me this week. I'm ready to work. That's why I'm here.

He stood up and walked toward the door. "Dude, you're going a hundred miles per hour and you need to slow down." The slamming screen door punctuated his sentence.

"I guess that was my first session," I told myself.

On the center of the table was a bottle of Deep Woods Off and Bob Seger's 1980 *Against the Wind* CD. Mosquitos have there own zip code in Louisiana, so I grabbed the insect repellant and headed out the door. Bob Seger would have to wait.

When you're used to moving fast, it's not easy to just 'be.' Your mind has a difficult time slowing down to experience all that is around you. But after a while, time slows and you begin to hear and see things that weren't there before. I guess fast paced living produces tunnel vision.

Killing four hours without distraction was grueling. I could hear the second hand on my wrist watch make her rounds.

After about three hours, I noticed a long boardwalk that weaved a path through the wetlands. It was well built. Each board perfectly positioned beside the other with nails spaced evenly apart. Wood and steel effortlessly united in their longing to lead me through the marsh. Every plank interconnected and yet incredibly independent with weight evenly distributed across the platform.

No single plank bore the burden of supporting the entire boardwalk. Weight was shared.

I bent down and ran my hand along the grains of the wood beneath my feet. Thousands of planks resting smooth and strong together. Their common load reminded me of the weight that rested solely upon my shoulders. I felt alone.

There's a heavy weight you carry when you're the lead guy. And it's easy for the smallest complaint or rejection to begin mounting an assault on your confidence as a leader.

Lunch that day was a plate of hummus with red peppers and slices of flatbread on the side. The food wasn't spicy, yet I found my eyes beginning to water as if I had swallowed a dozen fresh habaneros. I was emotionally raw.

Eddie returned as I swallowed my final bites of pita.

He sank into the chair across from me and asked, "How's it going?"

I spoke slower this time. Almost drugged. Intoxicated by rest. "I'm really good. I don't remember the last time I did that." Again, my eyes began to weep.

Trying to hide a tear from a therapist is like hiding crack cocaine from an addict. Somehow, they always find it. "I see that you're weeping. Tell me about that," Dr. Eddie said.

"I really don't know what's happening...I don't know." I felt the pressure of a billion tears behind my eyes mounting an attack and I didn't want to break.

Eddie thought for a second, then stood up and said, "Follow me."

I was hoping that he wasn't going to ask me to sand the boardwalk. That's where I would draw the line. I wasn't up for any Karate Kid shenanigans on this trip.

We walked across the freshly trimmed lawn to the edge of the woods next to the bayou. There sat a sun bleached wooden bench. It was a primitive creation, not one of those you would buy at a local box store. It was simple. Just two wooden poles on each end with a long board spanning the distance between them. The humidity was thick and the sun beat down upon my forehead.

Eddie motioned to the bench and said, "This is our 'Wailing Bench.' It was hand built to give people a place to release their pinned up emotion. In 2005, we had dozens of people who lost family members in Thailand's Tsunami sit on this very bench and wail. Later that year, when Hurricane

Katrina hit New Orleans, men and women who lost everything also sat on this bench and cried, wailed, and screamed at God."

He glanced at the bench, then looked back up at me and continued, "Now, it's your turn. Whatever emotion you have dammed up inside, this is the moment you have permission scream, wail and let it out."

He patted my shoulder and as he walked away, my tears dried up.

I was alone with the hot wailing bench. I sat down not knowing how to start. "Guess I should cry now," I said to myself.

Have you ever tried to make yourself cry? I'm not talking theater acting tricks, I mean the real deal. The overachiever in me felt pressure to produce, but I could not. I felt the pressure behind my eyes. Yet I couldn't squeeze out one single tear. Nothing. I was impotent.

After about 45 minutes in the sun, my blood began to boil and my sorrow turned to anger. I shot up out of my seat and squared off with my opponent. This damn bench would not defeat me.

Like a fighter facing his opponent I paced with nostrils flared standing toe to toe with this rag-tag piece of wood.

I was angry.

Pounding my fist in my hand, I fumed, "Bench, can't you see that I'm tired? Why do you have to pile on the pressure? I'm the one in this relationship that has to do all the work, not you. You just sit there doing nothing, with that smug look and impossible expectation that I perform. I hear you taunting me, 'What's wrong with you? Why can't you 'wail' like everybody else? You're a failure even here.'"

My rage crescendoed, "Well, stand in line, Bench. I'm about to let you down like I have everyone else in my life. Prepare for disappointment. I'm sick of trying to please everyone, including you...you lazy Bench. I cannot meet your expectations. I've got nothing. If I hadn't heard that touching story about you, I'd rip you to pieces right now. You son of a Bench."

I collapsed to the grass. Tearless. I was spent.

We were supposed to meet at 3:30 PM on the park bench near a large oak covered in Spanish moss. I arrived early. Too exhausted to move, I sat motionless. I could hear the buzzing of a mosquito in my right ear. I was a complete wreck. Eddie joined me on time and mirrored my rhythm. We both sat speechless.

As if on cue, a little brown squirrel ran right in front of us and took center stage. He stopped to scratch the ground for a nut. We weren't alone anymore. Eddie rested a calloused hand on my shoulder. The only thing that made me feel alive was the breath moving in and out of my lungs.

Eddie broke the silence with a whisper, "Look at that squirrel. You think he ever feels the same weight you feel?"

It was work just to lift my eyes. "Probably not." I replied.

I stared at the squirrel. How was it possible that a little brown creature was able to instinctively understand what it meant to be free? To live without expectation and know the pleasure of being enough.

And that's when it occurred to me, a squirrel's level of inner peace does not hinge on his ability to amass large quantities of nuts or his capacity to please others. He doesn't scurry around trying to rescue the world and is not driven to impress or please anybody. Even when that squirrel leaps from branch to branch or walks a tightrope at deathly heights, he doesn't seem panicked at all. Just free.

Squirrels just do what God created them to do. And that's enough.

As a church planter, my self-worth had been proportional to the size of my church. I couldn't breathe when my church wasn't growing. I felt underwater and my sinking ego desperately needed a massive organization to buoy it to the surface. I needed the church to make me okay.

I wonder if most pastors jump into ministry for a handful of the wrong reasons. Perhaps God leverages our brokenness to stir us to lead His church. Many leaders start out thinking the church will bring us wholeness and somehow fix us. We had hoped that a bigger building, a larger stage or a lineup of grateful people could somehow help us like the person we see in the mirror.

Fortunately, God loves us too much to let us continue to be fueled by our brokenness. At some point in the journey, God uses the struggles of leadership to purify our motives and fashion us into the likeness of Christ. And this purifying fire will set out to prove that only the grace of Christ has the power to make you enough.

And that's when I discovered, *the church is a terrible savior.*

## - STANDING EIGHT COUNT -

# BURNT. GRACE. HOPE...

*by Aaron Monts*

No one should ever have to write an obituary for their church. It's just not fair. Closing down a church is hard enough, difficult enough, painful enough. Yet, that's exactly what I had to do: IKON Christian Community 2008-2012. This is my story.

I stared through the windshield, no longer aware of the beauty of the crisp, Midwestern sunset. Perhaps I had become catatonic. My hands folded in my lap, slouched in the driver's seat. The three of us sat in the parking lot of Oklahoma Joe's BBQ in Kansas City. Their question hung heavy in the air, the weight of decision resting squarely on my shoulders alone.

"Aaron, what do you want to do? Shut it down or try and reboot?"

Shut it down? How in the world did we get here? I mean, we had everything we needed to succeed as a church plant in downtown San Francisco. In fact, I'd argue we had more than we needed to succeed! I had done everything I was supposed to do; everything that was required, recommended, and then some.

It was only a few months ago that we were featured prominently and positively in the New York Times. I had just finished a spread featuring our church in the "Power Edition" of San Francisco Magazine. Then a second and amazing article was written about us in the Bay Citizen, which was picked up nationally by the Huffington Post. We had all the free advertising and positive publicity you could ever ask for and imagine!

Before all the publicity, I prepared for church planting by doing a 14-month leadership residency with a leading, innovative, well respected church - even before doing a residency was the thing to do. My residency taught me a lot about leadership, myself, church planting strategies and encouraged me to risk. My residency led me into relationships and opportunities and experiences that I was able to lean into and lean on throughout the church planting journey. It was an amazing experience that truly prepared me better than anything else I could have experienced.

Our church was a part of national church planting organizations and partnered with two prominent, well regarded and respected networks with great churches in Boston, New York, Paris, El Paso, Miami, San Diego, Los Angeles, Chicago and beyond. Partnerships that made planting in the second most expensive city in the country financially possible. We had a great staff full of extremely smart, talented, sacrificial people who gave a lot of themselves to starting this new church.

We also had money. I don't mean to say that we were overflowing at the seams with cash, but often times churches face the decision to close because they simply cannot make it financially. That was not our story. We were sitting on solid financial footing and growing. In fact, we were well above the national average in church size and continued to add people to our community regularly.

We had it all. Notoriety. Preparation. Networks. Staff. Money. Growth.

*Shut it down? You can't be serious?*

I looked down at my hands, nervously rubbing them together; stalling for time, waiting for a spark of ingenuity that would make everything better, hoping for that Divine Spark that God would somehow intervene at this very moment and change their question, or better yet, change the reality that I was unwilling to face.

"Aaron. You're not well," Greg said from the backseat. "I love ya, bro, but you've gotta get real with yourself right now. Do you think you have it in you to reboot this thing?"

The reality is that shortly after my daughter was born I had taken a leave of absence from the church. I was exhausted. At thirty-three years of age, after more than five years of working to start this new church, I had come face-to-face with burnout. I was fried. And in my two-month absence, the church began to unravel because the staff and leaders were fried too.

I had reached an unhealthy existence. I didn't know what taking a day off looked like. I didn't know the term "vacation," let alone understand what Sabbath was or meant. I didn't understand the importance of rest, exercise, eating right, or simply taking care of oneself. I had become a mess and as a result, the demands I made on my staff and of my volunteer leaders grew to unfair and exhausting levels. My expectations were through the roof, so high that no one in their right mind could achieve them. Not only was I burnt out, but I was sowing burnout in everyone around me. I had created an unhealthy culture of performance and expectation and I kept raising the bar even though it was already out of reach; even for myself.

To get really real with you, this made me angry. Really angry. My already short fuse burned even shorter. Mad outbursts masked as passion became commonplace. People began to walk on pins and needles around me, fearful that at any moment I might explode. My world was crumbling around me, and I didn't realize it; I didn't recognize what was happening. All I knew was that I was angry and frustrated that things were not going the way I wanted them to. I couldn't get the traction that was expected of me because of our national exposure - and when you're already wiped out, this just piles it on and adds to the madness.

"Aaron, you're not well..." those words felt like salt in an already apparent and gaping wound. I bit my tongue. I really wanted to scream out, "Well Greg, you're G** D*** right I'm not well! What do you expect from me? I've given everything I have to this thing and yet it's still not enough!" I held it in and counted to 10. Just so you know, that whole, take a deep breath and count to 10-thing really only works in the moment, there's work you have to do down the line to truly get rid of the anger that is building up. You can't simply breathe it away.

As I rubbed my hands together I took stock of my life. What seemed like ages only took about a moment. I knew there was no way, in my condition, that I could jump back in and not only fix the challenges that we faced as a church, but reboot the church back to health. You cannot sow health when you yourself are not healthy. I knew I had nothing left to give. I was done. And in that moment, staring through the windshield in the parking lot of Oklahoma Joe's, the words crossed my lips, "It's done."

What's crazy, is that it took only two words.

Two words to dismantle everything I had worked for.
Everything our team had worked for.
Everything our church worked for.
Two words to end a dream that had lived in my heart for nearly a decade.
Two words.

It may have only taken two words but this was the hardest decision I have ever had to make, and it destroyed me. No one should ever have to write an obituary for their church and no one should ever have to make a decision like this.

Our management team took care of all the rigors and procedures of shutting down the church. They recommended that I stay away from everything and just rest. "Get well" was the prescription. And that's exactly what I did, although not completely by choice. I got sick.

For the next three months I was, for the most part, bed ridden. Unable to move. Through the stress of burnout, poor diet, not taking care of myself, my body had produced a kidney stone the size of a grape. (Yeah...a grape! It's okay to go to the fridge right now and look at a grape to see what I mean.) Surgery was on the horizon, but in the meantime I was left to lay in bed, forced to rest in a drug induced stupor. I was alone with my thoughts, a journal, and a 5-month old little girl.

I laid there and yelled at God...questioned God...hated God. Why on earth would He do something like this? And I don't just mean the chronic pain, I meant the church. Why would he close down something so beautiful? Why would he let me get to this place? How could he? Where was everyone? Why was I all alone? What could I have done differently? Why? How? Who? When? What? Where? All the questions. All the frustrations. All the anger. All the rage; poured out against God.

And then it happened. It all turned.


I turned on myself.
I pulled God out of the equation,
I realized everything was completely my fault.
My responsibility.
My failure.
The demise of the church rested on my shoulders and mine alone.


At the suggestion of my wife, I went to see a therapist. But before going, I had a few bits of criteria. I didn't want to sit with a Christian. I wanted to enter into a relationship with a therapist who would have no problem telling me how horrible of a person I was. How what I had done was the absolute worst thing in the world. I wanted to sit with someone who was going to beat me up and give it to me straight, without all of the "Christian fluff." Enter Dr. B, a well respected veteran therapist who had never sat with a church planter before. We sat together three times a week for the next 2 months as I laid everything out, as I walked through everything I did and failed at, over and over and over again. I tried to paint the worst possible picture of myself that I could, and when I felt like Dr. B wasn't reacting enough to the horrors, I painted an even worse picture.

Dr. B sat there with his legs crossed, notepad resting gently on his knee, lightly gripping his pen in his fist - a pen he never seemed to use by the way. He asked difficult questions, probing questions, piercing questions, the kinds of questions that get beneath the reality you're attempting to construct and straight into what actually was.

We dug deep into the hurt, the feelings of betrayal, the feelings of loss. We dug deep into the shame. I don't know if you know this or not, but there is a lot of shame associated with closing down a church plant. A lot of shame. For more than a year after the closing, I walked around with what amounted to a scarlet letter 'F' (for failure) on my chest. It's almost as if people didn't know how to talk to me anymore. Associations I had, people I thought were friends, they all up and vanished and I was left alone to process through this grief by myself.

Can I just put this out there? If you have a friend or an associate who just shut down their church, talk to them. Right now! Put down this book and fire off an email, send them a text, give them a call. Ask them how they are doing, talk about baseball or the amazingness that is the Golden State Warriors. It doesn't matter what you talk about really, just your call will make a difference. Don't try and put a silver lining on things, just let them know they aren't alone. Let them know that you care. And call them back in a week or two - then do it again and again and again. You may not understand what they're going through, and it doesn't matter, it's your presence that matters. It's sort of like the ancient Jewish practice of sitting

Shiva. We need people who will simply sit with us in the grief. You don't have to say anything; we just need you to sit with us.

Dr. B sat Shiva with me.

And then he broke up with me. *My therapist broke up with me.*

After 2 months, Dr. B looked at me with a piercing look full of grace and compassion, seriousness and intensity. It was one of those looks that felt like he was looking deep into my soul and trying to communicate with the core of my very being.

"Aaron, I want you to know that you're okay."

For the longest time I had been told that I was unhealthy, that I was damaged, that I was hurt and hurting others, all of which were true. Those sentiments had become my reality, they had fused themselves into my identity. And here, Dr. B looked at me and spoke new life, words of hope, words of affirmation, of a new identity into my soul. It was powerful. And then he told me, I didn't need him anymore. That I was free.

I wish that I had listened to him, but I proceeded to go through 3 more therapists all who arrived at the same conclusion much faster—because the work had already been done with Dr. B. Three more therapists in the course of a month broke up with me and told me I was "okay." I did the work. I worked to put new rhythms and practices into my life to not only grow, but to care for my soul. I worked to rest my identity and expectations into the hands of Jesus. I stumble through this, I fall flat on my face, and yet each and every time I get back up because of grace. I have experienced a grace unbelievable, and that has changed everything.

Sometimes I feel like I'm taking crazy pills.

Fast forward three years. That's the thought that seems to go through my head at different times these days. My family has recently moved to Seattle where I am beginning the work of planting a new church here, in partnership with a solid organization. The past three years have been a journey of restoration, a journey of reconciliation, a journey of healing, and it is now that I can say I'm not just okay, I am doing well.

God has rejuvenated me, he has given me a new vision and a new dream. That's sort of His thing, isn't it? Making all things new. There have been a lot of people who, in the past couple years, have since come alongside of me to pray with me, to pray for me, to walk with me and to speak life into me, to believe in me and help me to believe in the gifts that God has given me. There is hope on the other side of the scarlet letter. And no matter where you are, with God's grace, you too can get up off the mat.

## - STANDING EIGHT COUNT -

# IT'S ALRIGHT MA (I'M ONLY BLEEDING)

*by Derek Sweatman*

*Pointed threats, they bluff with scorn*
*Suicide remarks are torn*
*From the fool's gold mouthpiece the hollow horn*
*Plays wasted words, proves to warn*
*That he not busy being born is busy dying*
**Bob Dylan**, It's Alright Ma (I'm Only Bleeding)


I thought I was dying.

That's what a panic attack feels like. It feels like everything is ending, without your approval, and away from your control. I was sitting at home on a Friday morning, my daughter asleep in the next room, and it happened. Quickly. In an instant my whole body felt hot as fire, my heart rate went way up, and my mind did that thing where it convinced itself (and me) that everything was coming to an end.

I called someone to come and take care of my daughter. Then I called 911 and listened closely to the lady on the other end as she walked me through a checklist of clues. I gave her my address. My age. I told her my daughter was asleep in the next room. She asked me how old she was. I said she would turn one soon. We monitored my pulse. She had me look for aspirin. I didn't have any. More panic. She said the EMS was close. My kitchen suddenly looked messy. Breakfast still lingered. Dog food was on the floor. Dishes needed to be done. I wasn't ready to host people.

"The EMS are there."

"Thank you."

"You're gonna be okay, honey."

In the South you're still called honey, even by the 911 lady, even when you're dying.

I walked out front, and into the care of strangers. It was very quiet. They worked as a team. One helped me get my shirt off, two others attached all the wires to my chest, and one monitored the machine. Neighbors were now watching. My daughter was still asleep. The men talked quietly to each other. I felt fat, exposed, and embarrassed. One of the men, watching the data on the screen, put his hand on my shoulder. "You okay, buddy?"

"I don't know, that's why I called you." He laughed. After a few minutes they pulled the wires off, packed up the equipment, and three of them disappeared into the truck. The remaining one said to me, "Your readings are normal. But you're under some serious stress, we can all see that. It's protocol that you go to the hospital and have a complete workup, and I want to encourage you to do that."

The funny thing about ER triage is that "heart situations," even imagined ones, have dibs on getting a room. Hold your chest and you'll level up pretty fast. Within minutes I was taking another EKG test, giving lots of blood, and having an IV installed. It was going to be a long day. It was Friday. Sunday was coming. But something told me I wasn't preaching on Sunday.

Soon my wife arrived. She's a teacher. It was 50's day at her school. She looked like an extra from *Happy Days*. We sat there in that room, laughing at her outfit, and crying about whatever the hell it was that was going on with me. The doctor came in, sat on that stool with wheels, and rolled over to my bed. He said the same thing the EMS man said. "Derek, you're physically fine. But I want you to do everything you can to take some time off from your church. And if you need me to call your leaders or whomever makes those decisions, I'll do it. Oh, and you're pretty dehydrated." He left. I waited for my discharge papers. The nurse leaned down and said, "Honey, it's going to be okay."

Sabbath.

It feels like a death.

A lot of things go dark on the Sabbath. It's a blackout of production, and worst, the need to produce. In the original command we find God imposing a value of temporary uselessness upon a nation whose enslaved identity had been predicated on their usefulness to the Pharaoh. Their work was essential to life. Stop working, stop living. There is no rest in slavery, physically or otherwise. Apart from oppression and control, slavery's mission is production. And, like a gift, God opened up a new way for His people. He set rest against production, a little 24-hour resistance movement to keep the week honest and centered. No longer would His people be defined by their work. Rest would give meaning to activity. Sabbath would now have the wheel.

There's no mistaking the direction of the Genesis 1 story, how it moves from chaos to rest. It starts with disorder, with ruins, with creation dismembered and nearly nonfunctioning. In that image of the Spirit of God hovering over the untamed waters of fear and scarcity and breakage, we see God's readiness to reorganize and renew what's gone adrift in His world. The first picture we get of the Spirit is in the first riff of the Bible, and we learn straightaway that the Spirit brings order and rest into our worlds. And those words, "it was evening and it was morning," the bass drum of the story's music, the rhythm of the march towards Day Seven, after which there is no "evening or morning." Day Seven is the point. God's history is headed to a Day Seven realm, a time when all things are complete, when (and where) there is Shalom, Shabbat Shalom, rest and peace (and the peace of rest).

The Sabbath keeps this future in view. Of the Sabbath, the Jews have a saying, that the day itself is a taste of the world to come, "olam ha'ba." When we rest, we are rehearsing for eternity. Sabbath is rehearsal. When we cut ourselves off from the world's need for us to be productive, we not only speak against that particular social understanding of one's identity, but in the process we remind ourselves of whose world this really is, and that we are not obligated to keep the world on its axis.

To be clear, there is no opposition between being and doing. We often think this is so, guilty of notions that to *do* is religious, and to *be* is godly. This is not the message of the Sabbath. It is not a counter argument against the rest of the week, as though everything leading up to it was worthless and therefore separated from God's best for our lives. Instead, the Sabbath allows us freedom to stop creating, and to remember the Creator. It gives us the time needed to rest from "making things happen", and the space to remember the great cause of all things. There is a deeply embedded lesson learned only in the Sabbath rest, that to stop working doesn't lead to a life of less.

So much of what informs and shapes my life is located in the things I actually do. But I had forgotten the value of nothingness. Life needs room. An empty room. Space to sit alone, undisturbed, and timeless. There is an important void to seek, and then, to protect, a Sabbath from the need to fill what feels empty. It's good to enter that holy space and time, one in which

Heschel says, "eternity utters a day." Before I do anything, it's important that I do nothing at all, a divine and wonderful delinquency.

I had forgotten all of this.

For several weeks I didn't go to work. I didn't do anything. Our family didn't go to church. Anywhere. Sundays were different. We slept in. We ate breakfast together. I went for runs and bike rides. We played music. Watched TV. Read things. Skipping church was nice. I started to understand the attraction of such a practice. I recommend it. I also got help. My doctor put me on medication. He gave my wife and I the keys to his condo on Hilton Head, Island, and said, "Go, relax. Start over. Again."

I look back on that season often. It was a hinge for me. Everything swung in a new direction. I still have moments. I still have panic attacks. The doctor said they would happen more often. You have one, you'll have another. That's how it works. The first one primed the pump. But my team knows. My elders check on me often. My staff deals with the ups and downs. My church is patient with me. My family protects me, and reminds me that the Sabbath was made for us, not us for the Sabbath. It is a gift, an invitation into a place where we're allowed to let everything go. And that's the trick.

*There is a day*
*when the road neither*
*comes nor goes and the way*
*is not a way but a place.*
Wendell Berry

## - STANDING EIGHT COUNT -

# GOOD

*by Jonathan Williams*

I was 12 years old when I saw New York Islander defenseman, Jeff Norton absolutely pummel an opposing player on the Philadelphia Flyers. The fans at the Nassau Coliseum went crazy. This is what watching a hockey game was all about. There was shouting, jumping, plenty of cursing, and a few fans banging on the plexiglass that separated the stands from the hockey players on the ice. I stood up and shouted too, exerting some of that 12-year old pubescent angst deep within my body. I looked over and watched my dad, a hockey fan, content in his seat, legs crossed, politely clapping for all that was witnessed. I stared at my dad and then at the other men in the coliseum. My dad wasn't jumping out of his seat, cursing or punching the plexiglass. Was it because he was a pastor? Was it because he was different?

It was a fleeting moment.

I didn't think about that game again until 22 years later. I thought about that game again on the day that my father told me that he was living a lie. My father flew to New York. We sat in my living room. What was it my father would tell me? He was leaving ministry? He and my mother were divorcing? Did he cheat on his taxes? Was he gay?

It was there in my living room that my father told me that he was transgendered.

Cheating on taxes would have been so much better.

My father explained that he always felt as though he should be female. There's a medical term for what my dad was experiencing. It was called body dysmorphia. My father revealed that over the next few months there would be many changes that would allow him to live life as a woman and there would be other changes that would allow her to live life as she had always hoped. She would begin dressing differently. There were hormones and surgeries.

I know it sounds strange, but for some reason those words from my dad took me back to that night in Nassau Coliseum: legs crossed, clapping politely, so different. I thought about my father who took me to games. I thought about my dad and the many moments we talked man to man while hiking in the Rocky Mountains. I thought about the thousands of times I called my dad to ask advice or to talk about the Mets. My dad was my friend, my mentor, my hero.

My dad was no longer my dad. It felt like the relationship I had with my father was a lie.

I was devastated.

And I had just started a church.

We were only three months into the life or our church and my dad flew to New York to tell me about her transition. How would I function? Did I need to quit? I couldn't tell anyone at church. My father wasn't "out" yet and the information was sensitive. I couldn't tell my staff or any of my supporting churches.

I felt alone.

I lied to everyone and said that I was okay. "My challenges are nothing out of the ordinary," I would say. This was a battle I fought on my own. It was a battle I was losing. I found it hard to get out of bed. I started drinking too much. I was depressed and angry. I had little energy for interactions and conversations. On Sunday mornings I'd be crying in the green room wondering how I was going to give a message of hope to my fledgling church community when I had no hope myself. I didn't believe in God.

One day a staff member said, "Jonathan, where are you? Are you even here? Are you with us?" I was laying on a couch in the office regretting the fact that my dad's crossed legs at a hockey game didn't clue me in sooner. If I had known then, I wouldn't be going through this pain now. I'd be able to focus on our church, on growth, and on sharing the love of Christ with no limitations. I'd have engaged with my staff in positive ways. I wouldn't have had emotional breakdowns when there was a missed email or a volunteer who failed to show up on time.

On one occasion, a few church community members came to meet with me. They were displeased with our worship and ready to move on from our church. I sat and listened but could only think of how incredibly selfish they were. I wanted to yell and scream, "My dad is a woman and you're leaving the church over the style of our worship? Get the F*ck out then!"

I fought my way through the good meetings too. There was the meeting where our staff celebrated the fact that we raised and gave away over $100,000 to local organizations. It was hollow. I didn't care. I didn't want to be in that meeting. I didn't want to celebrate.

I met with new attenders and new leaders. I led a small group. I stopped crying in the green room just long enough to preach a decent sermon each Sunday. I approved budgets that set our church up for success. Our church grew quickly. I got to hear stories about people who never thought they would encounter Jesus again until they found our church. I heard other stories about how the Gospel finally made sense to someone who always considered themselves an atheist. I celebrated each of these stories with hollow eyes and a hollow heart. I wondered if I would ever encounter Jesus again.

As far as I was concerned, Jesus was dead.

I would go home and tell my wife that life was unfair. It made no sense. I was scarred, battered, bruised, and I wasn't the person to lead this church. The pain was too great. I physically and emotionally had nothing left to give, and my friend, my mentor, my hero couldn't help me. She was going through her own transition.

And then, in the darkest night of my mourning, I learned about the Hebrew word, *Tov*.

In fact, when we read the creation narrative in Genesis, each time that God says, "It's good" it's translated from the Hebrew word, "*tov*."

The word, "*tov*" doesn't mean the same thing as the English word, "good." It doesn't carry the same implications of mood or morality. Instead, "*tov*" literally means, "for its intended purpose."

When God says that creation is good, God is saying that it's created for its intended purpose. That means that "good" doesn't always mean life will be okay. In fact, when God says that something is *tov*, there is usually light, growth, and birth followed by darkness, pain, and death. *Tov* means that the fullness of life often comes with pain. It means that we won't always have the answers we want. It means that our shouts of, "Why God?" will feel like they're falling upon deaf ears. But it's "Good," which means that creation will work according to its intended purpose. Sometimes that purpose means there is devastating pain. But "*tov*" also means that pain will turn from darkness to light and from death to resurrection.

And if that's the case, then it was okay for me to be vulnerable. It was okay to be sad. It was okay to mourn my father. I was free to be angry. I was allowed to cry in the green room. I could tell my staff. I could let them comfort me. I didn't have to be a perfect leader. I realized that the pain I was feeling over my dad's transition was, "*tov*." It was for its intended purpose. My pain was good. It was righteous. It was bringing about resurrection.

It was time to tell my church.

During the season of Lent, I talked through the pain of my father's transition. I talked about the fact that it's good, it's *tov*, to be sad, angry, devastated, hollow. It's for its intended purpose.

And what was that purpose?

I'm a better pastor with a unique wisdom. I find I'm more gracious to the pain of others. I am able to live deep within the mystery of Christ rather than trying to give all of the answers. I've met amazing people who call my church their home. I've been able to reach out to my father and begin the process of reconciling our relationship. I've found the space to truly love my father. She's a wonderful woman and an incredible friend.

There are stories that our community was afraid to share before, but see that there is beauty in them now. I get the privilege of hearing, "I was afraid to share my pain and doubt but I see that there is a God at work in it."

Our church has become a place where vulnerability matters. We share in one another's burdens. We're willing to listen to one another's stories and show one another grace. We are a church that is willing to ask the hard questions, be angry, live in the pain, and fully know that this is good, *tov*, for its intended purpose. There is growth, love, and grace to come.

I still wish that my dad crossing his legs and clapping politely during a hockey fight would have clued me in earlier. I wouldn't wish that devastation on anyone in their first year of church planting. I still have that scar, a scar which runs deep and continues to heal. I still have that pain. I'm not sure that it will ever go away. I'm not sure it has to go away.

My pain is *tov*. My father's transition is *tov*. The vulnerability of our ministry is *tov*. The uncertainty, anger, sadness, hope, and joy are all *tov*.

They're for their intended purpose.

# WHAT DO YOU WANT TO PAY

*by Nate Bush*

At a breakfast meeting, with a network leader overseeing the finances for my 18 month old church, he paused after a sip of coffee and said, "You are out of money. What do you want to pay?" At that moment, I cursed a lot. I didn't really curse before church planting, but somehow the process has left my vocabulary longing for darker and more crushing words. You need the gospel to plant a church. The gospel teaches you that at the core of you, there is nothing left but inability. If you were able, Christ would not have to live for you. But staring at your inability is a practice of such vulnerability that shame would crush you with its dark fist if it were not for the gospel telling you of Christ's worth imparted to you.

Every planter will gaze at their own inability, face to face. My inability was financial support. I was trying to raise money in 2009 and 2010 at the height of the economic crisis. For instance, we sold our house in 2010 for $80,000 less than we paid for it. Our fundraising goal for the church plant was $500,000. We raised $135,000. Over a three year period.

Still, God said, go. We went. And it hurt really bad.

Our bank account was at zero. My wife and I lent the church $10,000. That kept the doors open. The staff got paid. However, my morale was hemorrhaging angrily. The church was not aware of how bad it was, and I was trying really hard to keep everyone optimistic about the future. After all, God called us to this mission, right?

Crisis always puts "calling" under the bright light of doubt. I was beginning to believe that it was my arrogance, not God's calling, that led us out to New Mexico. I was sure Albuquerque was my desert to die in. In this Exodus narrative, I went from feeling triumphal like Moses, to grumbling like the Israelites. There was little hope of manna from heaven.

I was radically saved by Jesus in bible college. I started my college years as an art student. After my conversion, I immediately gravitated toward Francis Schaeffer. However, it was not the writings of Francis Schaeffer that met me in my time of angry-despair; it was Edith Schaeffer. The Lord brought to mind Edith Schaeffer's book The *Life of Prayer*. I first read this book directly following my conversion. In that great book, Edith tells of their missionary journey to the Swiss Alps to set up their thinking ministry called the *L'abri*. Edith recalls praying for resources, God's miraculous provision, and a life of dependency upon God. As a brand new believer, this book struck me. I remember saying, "I am glad there are people who live like this, but I don't plan on being one of them!"

The Lord spoke to my wife and I very specifically the day we decided to plant New City Church. We were reading through the Bible together, though we were reading different reading plans. That morning we were both in Joshua 3. In the background noise of Joshua 3 there are whispers. "Be strong and courageous" whispers. The phrase, "I will not leave you or forsake you," floats softly upon your subconscious. Joshua is being told to cross the Jordan like Moses crossed the Red Sea. Only the miraculous stoppage of water doesn't happen right before their eyes. The water was stopped, "far away" in Adam. God had already prepared the way for the calling. However, Joshua could not see it. We tried to make Joshua's faith our faith. We couldn't see how God was already working, but we wanted to trust Him.

Our first Sunday was Easter 2010. On a Sunday in July of 2010, our offering total? $20. In this Promise Land narrative, I was losing the courage of Joshua and feeling more like the fearful spies of Numbers 13. I thought this is the "land that devours" its pastors. I day dreamed about driving a beer truck.

By the start of 2011, we were $20,000 in the red. Our per capita giving was $14. I was not living a dream. Maybe it was a nightmare. A nightmare might have been better at that time. You wake up from nightmares. Everyday I woke up to the same dark story.

During this season, we were growing. People were being converted. We were multiplying groups. We were raising up leaders. It was not all bad. However, we started a church for the lost and broken. The lost and broken don't give, and many can't give without serious and involved life adjustments. In many ways, we were accomplishing our goals. Funding those goals was the issue. I would get really angry about this. I would look at our church on Sunday and I knew we were killing it (in the best way). I was really proud of the community that God was developing. This made the lack of funding so much more maddening. I really believed in what we were doing.

The loaves and the fish gave me strength. There was a day in history that Jesus fed over 5,000 people with a little bit of bread and fish. The disciples see the need of the people and apply conventional wisdom. Jesus, however, applies a deeper kind of wisdom. The disciples could not see the arithmetic of Jesus. Five loaves and two fish cannot feed 5,000 men. Jesus does math differently.

In this story Jesus does not pressure the disciples to give anything more than they have. Jesus says something like, "Just give me what you have." This is what the Holy Spirit kept telling me. "Just give me what you have." Sometimes the Holy Spirit sounds like a drunk friend. Experience was teaching me to shut down this fanciful, "Holy Spirit" talk. That's what I thought. It's a bad idea to learn from a half-baked experience.

I gave in to the Holy Spirit. I gave God all that I had. Apparently, God is good at doing a lot with a little. After all, he did make *everything* out of *nothing*. I talked to the church. Our per capita giving rose the next week from $14 to $34. We started hosting mission teams. We made $50,000 that summer through mission teams. We ended the next year in the black.

There has not been a season of explosive growth. There have been steady seasons of God's provision. I curse less. I have more faith. I want to believe the miraculous is possible. I still default to conventional wisdom. God is providing. Everyone is provided for. And there is a little bit left over.

Our stories are always God's story. God is redeeming his world that is lost and broken by sin. He is redeeming my broken story. My life is currently in the progress of redemption. I can't hurry God's redemption story. That's not in my power. I can, however, submit to redemption as a process. One act of submission was giving our Easter offering away, especially when it hurt. This discipline became a value, a value of generosity.

Here's how it played out. We built out a store front. It used to be a Tuesday Morning store. There was a pole in the middle of where our auditorium was to be. To move that poll would cost us $20,000. That was the exact amount we had committed to a local elementary school. The previous year we met with the administration of Mission Avenue Elementary School. We were giving them our Easter offering of $20,000. As sometimes happens in generosity, the principal questioned our agenda. We assured her of our agenda-less love. (I am really glad we had earned her trust.) She believed us. Francis, the principal, dreamed of a mentor program. A tear began to build as she told us of the needs of her school. We started the program. I really wanted to see this mentor club continue. But I really hated that pole. We could not do both.

So we have a pole in the middle of the auditorium.

The pole reminds me of God's constant provision. And my constant need for his provision. It also reminds me that redemption is a process. In the perfect auditorium there would not be a pole. The world is not perfect. The whole world is still crying out in anticipation of its perfect renewal. Because we chose the mentor program and not the pole, we now have something greater than a mentor program.

The mentor program is called *Shine*. Now *Shine* organizes churches in our city to better love schools. *Shine* is holding a conference hosted by the public school system and local churches, together, rallying around the cause of children in our state. New Mexico is consistently last in education in our country. That stupid pole is now providing for, I believe, hundreds of matches between schools and churches who are innovating great ways to better love kids in need.

God's redemption plan for New City Church included a lack of funding. It was our lack of funding and constant need that slowed us down and helped us to realize that we did not "need" everything that we thought we needed. We could live on less as a church. We could give more as a church. We didn't have to get the fanciest building in the city. Instead, we get to give great and wonderful gifts to our city. Our auditorium has a pole in it. But our city has schools that are better loved.

In 2016, we are launching a Spanish-speaking church. It's going to be hard. I might start cursing again. We can't afford it. Yet the Holy Spirit says, "Give me what you have." There is a whisper saying, "Be courageous." I am starting to believe that God does not forsake me. May the Lord do what he pleases.

# THROWING IN
## THE TOWEL
### ROUND FOUR

## - THROWING IN THE TOWEL -

# A STORM AND A SHIPWRECK

*by Jerel Law*

I studied the painting on the wall, fidgeting in my chair in flat silence, trying to figure out if it was too late to break for the door and run for it. It was. I'd already paid my sixty dollars to Roger, and now he sat, studying me as I looked away, perfectly comfortable with neither of us saying anything.

I was anything but. He had asked a question - some question that counselors ask - and I honestly can't remember it. What I do remember is the painting on his wall.

A boat in a storm. Like the one Jesus was in – the one Jesus fell asleep in – while the storm raged around him. While his disciples panicked. Well, more than panicked – some of them no doubt were planning their escape. Could I swim for it? Could I make it back to shore alive? Others had likely already given up on that small hope, images of their moms, dads, maybe girlfriends, filling what they were sure would be their final thoughts. They'd seen storms like this before. They had heard tales of this sea. But they'd never been in one themselves…at least, not like this. Based on the reality of the storm that enveloped them, they could see no real way out.

"It's like we were in a boat," I began, a slight quiver in my voice that I tried to steady. "The five of us were cruising along. The water was smooth, the sky blue, and we were laughing, probably at something Luke, our youngest wild little boy, was doing. And then, with no warning, this storm blew in."

Roger nodded slowly. "Like in the picture?"

"Yeah," I said. "Except that instead of us being in the boat, it feels like we all got thrown out, the boat sank, and the kids and I are holding onto whatever scrap of wood we could find big enough to float. And I'm looking around frantically for her, but I can't find her, no matter how hard I look, how loud I call out her name. It's just me, the kids, and the wreckage."

"And Susan?" Roger whispered.

"Susan's gone."

My mind opened another file from the hard drive. Three years before, February of 2008. Sitting on our leather sofa in our family room, a few hours after the doctor had called to deliver the news. Previously, I had thought those phone calls only happened in movies. But no, this was real life, as real as it gets, and the doctor had called, direct and apologetic, delivering the news: breast cancer.

We spent the first couple of hours vacillating between "Holy crap!" and "We can beat this!", but finally sunk into the sofa, exhausted. American Idol was on, and a girl began singing, "Yesterday, all my troubles seemed so far away…" As much as I'd been trying to hold it together, to "be strong", the words landed punches unguarded and Susan and I crumpled into the cushions, holding each other more and more tightly as the tears finally began to flow.

Susan and I met in 1990 during my freshman year of college at the University of North Carolina at Chapel Hill. Literally, she was leading worship when I first laid eyes on her. Which as it turns out, was God's funny way of foreshadowing the life we would have together. We dated for four years, and were married in May of 1995. I did student ministry after graduation, but knew after awhile that God was calling me to help lead a church that was unapologetically targeting seekers, not the already-convinced. And quite possibly, to plant a church.

Eventually, in 2004, that's what we did, on the north side of Charlotte, North

Carolina. It was wonderfully terrifying, either that or terrifyingly wonderful, depending on your perspective. God was faithful, He moved in people's lives, not the least of which was our own. Susan and I were forging new territory, and doing it together, all with our three little ones in tow.

One of my lasting memories was in 2006. Luke was a baby military-crawling along the school hallways where the church was renting space, while our setup crews rolled carts around him. Or when Christopher, my middle child, knocked out his front tooth playing with a rolling cart after church one day in the YMCA where we had started to meet. People came to know Christ for the first time in that setting. Some of my best friends now, John and Stephanie, found a relationship with Jesus through this church, after years of nominal faith, if any at all.

Planting a church was incredibly difficult. We saw people come, and then saw others go. We had friends we thought would be in it with us for the long haul, abandon the vision (and to be honest, abandon us) for the greener grass of different churches with ministries further along, or with buildings, or more momentum. This was in some ways harder for Susan. Our defensiveness kicks in to an especially high degree when our spouses are threatened.

The church had a hard time with traction. We began to experience our share of financial difficulties in 2007 and 2008 as the national economy came crashing down. People took pay cuts, or moved out of state to chase jobs...all of which affected giving, and us.

And then, the diagnosis came.

It's amazing how clarifying crisis can be. Want to find out what you care about? Want to really know what is important? Just introduce crisis into the situation and see what happens.

My priority had always been my marriage, but it was so easy to let other things get in the way...good things. Like the church, like our family, even our kids. If my priorities weren't in order before, they got there fast. Susan began to go through chemotherapy, surgery, and radiation. When she had a recurrence in 2009, she went through it all again. That would go on for three solid years. Life had opened up a sinkhole underneath us, but we were determined to do our best; to be as faithful as we could be, to parent our kids well, to love one another selflessly, and maybe most of all, to fight to stay above ground.

And fight we did.

In the summer of 2009, though, it became apparent that the church was facing some significant issues. This wasn't news to me or anyone on our leadership team. As I pulled away to pray that summer, for the first time, I felt something different from God as it related to this church – a release from the calling. I returned from the break and began to talk and pray with our leadership about ending public services. It was sad, but very peaceful. I don't understand it all, because I believe we did a lot of things right - as far as the textbooks go, anyway. But it was clear that this season of ministry was over for us. So in August 2009, we held our last public service together.

I'll be honest – yes, it was devastating at the time. But I had bigger issues going on, and because of that, what could have felt like the end of the road, or end of my career, or the end of lots of things...wasn't. Susan continued treatments, and I received what I needed most – a forced sabbatical. I was toast...completely burned out, and I knew it. I needed to rest, to simplify, to refocus, and give all my attention to my wife and kids. And in one of the darkest times at that point for us, God - the surprising, mysterious, confusing, and gracious God that He is - came bearing gifts.

I seem to appreciate most of His gifts in retrospect. Maybe the more spiritual can sense them in real time. I began to write a book during that time, at Susan's great encouragement. Two years later I received an email from a publisher who wanted the book I had written. That email would change the course of my life. What I thought was going to be a three-month ministry break - which in my mind would lead to another pastoral position somewhere - became four, then six, then eight months. I was having multiple conversations with pastors and churches that wanted to hire me but didn't have the money. It was 2009, and everyone's budget had flatlined.

I complained to God a lot in those days. I didn't understand why…why did we start this church? Why did we have to shut it down? And of course the biggest question – why did Susan get cancer? And my more immediate question – why can't I find a job?

It was only later that I got a glimpse of an answer. Susan's health really spiraled out of control in the fall of 2010. The cancer had found cracks and crevices to do anything it could to squeeze through the doorways we'd tried so desperately to seal. It pressed itself into her body from all sides, until all defense was rendered useless.

On January 1, 2011, Susan died.

She was there, and then she was gone. I realize that is an obvious statement, but there is a harsh reality to that kind of loss that you can't prepare yourself for, no matter how certain you are that it's coming. So there we were, floating in this vast ocean together, uncertain and untethered.

Over the next months I came to understand that the time I'd spent with her: going to every appointment, walking with her through this awful thing as much as I could – time I had because I wasn't working – couldn't have happened otherwise. If we were going a hundred miles an hour with this church plant, or if I'd taken another job, or if we'd moved…none of it would have been possible. Even though at the time I desperately wanted to be on to the ministry that was next – I felt like I needed that. The fact those opportunities didn't happen...well, as it turns out, that was a gift to me.

To spend those last precious days with Susan is time I will never, ever get back. I'm not one to claim that cancer is a gift. Perhaps I'm just not there yet. But let me say this – and I say it with the lightest touch on this chisel possible – some things we don't view as God's gifts are just that. Lest we all forget, He is in the redemption business. And as a pastor, I especially need to remember that is not just for others. It's for me. For my children. His promise is to redeem all of this.

Aren't there things that are true regardless of what we want to believe about them at any given moment? The truth about God unearthed in the story of Joseph and his brothers in Genesis is one I have found to steady me more and more as the days go on.

## YOU INTENDED TO HARM ME, BUT GOD INTENDED IT FOR GOOD TO ACCOMPLISH WHAT IS BEING DONE, THE SAVING OF MANY LIVES.
### - GENESIS 50:20 -

I sense God whispering in my ear on a regular basis in regards to these words.

Where are the kids and I now? We have moved forward. We haven't "gotten over it" (I'm not sure you do), we are just moving forward. We miss Susan every day. We are marked by this thing, and we are different because of it. But we are laughing, and studying, and playing music, and playing basketball, and hanging out with friends. We're working, and writing, and even church planting again (yikes!). We're grappling with this tragedy in our own ways. We're living. And we're finding God to be more than we ever thought possible.

In short, I guess you could say it like this: we've built another boat.

# - THROWING IN THE TOWEL -

# DEATH: THE FINAL BLOW

*by Jon McClarnon*

Every Sunday morning, I walk through the main doors of our auditorium and my attention goes to one very specific place on the stage. I wouldn't even say this is a conscious decision. I just can't help it. Something happened in that spot that changed me. Something happened there that changed our church.

Every Sunday morning I also walk through every part of the building before anyone arrives. When I walk through the back doors of the auditorium and into the first room behind our stage, I picture a small group of people standing in prayer.

If I allow myself the time to stop and stand there I can almost audibly hear Bill pray, "Lord, help us to be still and know you are God."

Bill was a very quiet and unassuming kind of man. Soft spoken and extremely genuine, he never wanted to draw attention to himself. But there was something about the way he prayed those 11 words that was noticed by several people in that circle that day.

On this particular day, my wife was singing in the band. As they get ready to strike the opening chords, she jokes with Ron, the worship leader, that Bill is late to his keyboard. They all share a laugh as Bill finally takes his place just in time for the start of *Your Grace is Enough*.

I've taken my place on the front row where I typically sit. Hard as I try, I have difficulty trying to maintain a healthy balance between participating in worship and critiquing what is happening. For one, unless you're doing a scissor kick during a guitar solo, I tend to get a little nervous when band members start moving around on the stage.

We're still in the first song and Bill takes a couple steps away from the keyboard. He then turns back. I can't help but notice when a guy, who doesn't want to be noticed, does something he doesn't normally do. He takes a few more steps away from the keyboard again.

"What is he doing?" I think to myself as I watch. Maybe a cord had come loose on a piece of equipment. It was not uncommon in our shared rented facility for us to have some technical problems from time to time. A loose cord would make sense. Bill did something different.

Bill went down on his knees and fell on his face.

My first thought was that he tripped because there was a lot of stuff on that stage. However, when he didn't get up immediately, I assumed he had fainted. That wasn't the case either. Bill rolled over on his back and pulled his right arm to his chest. I knew this was serious.

But nobody moved. And nobody seemed to think twice.

The band was playing out the first song and really enjoying themselves. Because Bill was positioned behind all the other instrumentalists, no one noticed he was lying across the back of the stage.

I wasn't entirely sure what was happening but I knew standing on the front row wasn't the place to be. I ran onto the stage, skipping most of the steps, taking the most direct route to where Bill lay. The band continued to finish out the opening song, not entirely sure what I was up to.

I bent down on my right knee and put my left hand behind his neck to help support his head, and with my right hand I held onto Bill's right hand. Turning over my left shoulder I yelled to my friend Lee on the congas, "Get the Doc!"

The Doc has been a friend of mine for 15 years, and while he's technically an orthopedic surgeon, he's the first person that comes to my mind. I'm trying to stay calm and relaxed as possible so that I can think clearly. Bill's eyes are closed but he's breathing. I know this because he utters something in a soft but wheezy voice. I feel like he wants me to know what's going on in case we might ever have a question. "Heart attack".

Meanwhile, the band has stopped. The drummer has called 911. The Doc has now joined me on stage with Bill.

Then Bill's wife, Debbie, walks into the service.

None of the other 75 adults in the room arrived late this day. I am pretty sure this had never happened in the previous 5 years of our church.

Just Debbie.

Debbie walks into the auditorium to see her husband lying on the stage surrounded by a handful of people. As she joins the group on the stage, along with one of our members who is a nurse, I turn my attention to the crowd. "What do we do with these people?" I thought in the moment.

I make an announcement to remain calm and to please pray for Bill. I invite a couple of our guys to come up front to lead the church in prayer and I ask our guitar player to play something softly in the background.

I turn to Kurt - the Doc - and ask, "What do you need?"

"I need those guys to get here," was his response.

And they did. The first responders and paramedics arrived fairly quickly. I moved to the side and let the medical experts take over. I let those leading in prayer continue to pray. I took a seat on the front row, praying for Bill and thinking about what we should do from this point on. The questions began to pour into my mind...

How do we care for Bill?

How do we care for Debbie? It was her birthday.

What are the first and second time guests thinking?

How do we bring perspective to a crowd when we're not even sure what we're dealing with in the moment?

And then there are the teenagers. I have three and they're all seated on the front row.

Some 30 minutes after we began the service, Bill was taken out to the ambulance. At this point, we knew nothing for sure. Only that he would continue to receive treatment in the parking lot and be transported to the hospital.

We decided to abbreviate our service that morning. I was starting a new series teaching on the "Lord's Prayer" and we had backloaded the day with worship. I gave a 15 minute version of the message and we were going to wrap up with 2 or 3 songs.

At some point during those closing songs I got word; "They're still in the parking lot." They wanted me to know that we would need to send people out another exit and navigate the parking lot.

I knew hearing those words meant something much more serious was happening.

My thoughts solidified when Debbie came back into the auditorium while we were singing. She made her way down to the open space between the front row and the stage. She sang with everything she had. She lifted her hands in worship. She swayed and danced and was the very picture of someone who was surrendering everything she could to God in that moment.

And I knew.

We started the morning with a worship service and we ended it by ushering a man into heaven and God's presence. There was hardly any distance between here and there in that moment.

Bill was only 54 years old.

When we dismissed that morning, people continued to jump in wherever needed. Everyone pulled together. I don't think I was ever more proud of our church than on that day.

My wife and I, along with a couple of Bill and Debbie's close friends spent the rest of the afternoon at the hospital trying in any way to help absorb the tragic shock of the day. That night at the house, we planned to meet up on Monday to talk through the details of a funeral service.

When I walked into my local coffee shop on Monday morning, people were already buzzing with the news of what had happened. People I didn't even know were coming up to me and asking how I was doing. Two guys I've never met before prayed over me while I sat at my table drinking my coffee and trying to digest what I'd experienced in the last 24 hours.

That same day I went to a sandwich shop for lunch and it was a repeat of the morning encounters. Later that night, I was playing pickup basketball at a church 20 minutes away and before we began playing, the organizer asked that we pray for a church that experienced a tragedy. He was a friend of Bill's.

Tuesday I got a call from a pastor 45 minutes away. More encounters at lunch. People at dinner. Everywhere I went people had heard about Bill's death and wanted to ask questions, most without adequate words beyond, "Wow."

I was even running on the treadmill at my gym later that night when someone walked over, got on the treadmill next to me just so he could say, "I heard a crazy rumor..." Everywhere I went it was one person after another saying, "I heard what happened."

On one of those days between Bill's death and his funeral it became clear to me, "God I see what you're doing. You are using all things so that people will talk about you." Bill's life had everyone talking. Some about Bill. Some about the church. Mostly all about God.

That's the way Bill would have wanted it. The first time I had lunch with Bill it was clear that he wanted his life to make a difference. He wanted to tell the greater story of God by how he lived. He wanted to make his days count by listening to God and following God. It turns out that his death may have been the moment in which he drew the biggest audience to tell the story of God to more people that he could have ever imagined.

On Thursday, four days after Bill passed away, we held the first funeral ever in the life of our church. The place was packed. I estimated well over 300 people showed up. Evidence that Bill's life had touched so many others. Debbie wanted to make sure we put the "fun" into funeral so we had our full band lead us in a worship celebration.

In my message I wanted to remember Bill and his life and yet I also wanted to challenge everyone there to give however many days they had left to telling the story of God. I love the way it was phrased in the obituary: "Bill went to be with the Lord during worship on June 3, 2012."

How cool is that?

The next question for me became, "So what do we do on June 10th?" How do you deal with the fact that an entire room full of people watched a man die in front of them?

I knew there were at least two giant takeaways.

First, I had to plead with people to make every minute of their life count. Anyone who experienced the Sunday before needed very little in the way of coercing. After all, last Sunday there were 7 people on the stage and this Sunday there were only 6. I told our people that I would never have to build a case again for the fact that life is short. They could never accuse me again of playing on anyone's emotions to get a response. "You are witnesses. And when you've seen what you've seen and experienced what you've experienced, you can not remain the same."

Second, I knew I had to challenge our church to a whole new level of urgency. If life is short and people spend forever somewhere, then as a whole, we had to share that with anyone and everyone who would listen. I said, "This place should be full next week because you had to tell somebody."

For five years I felt we had done everything in our power to help facilitate growth in the church. I sat down one day and outlined all the things we had tried. It was 3 legal pages long.

We did mailers and hung door hangers. We were involved in every kind of community event we could find. We worked with local schools and served in shelters. We touched the world in Kenya and Mexico. On our 2nd anniversary we held an Easter event that drew 1,200 people. Not one of those 1,200 people - as far as we know - ever came to the church as a result.

For five years I struggled with our church's lack of growth. I questioned what we were doing and wondered what the future held. Were we really making a difference?

"God, is this how you're going to do it? You're going to use Bill's death as the catalyst for growth?" I thought.

This is the part of the story where I am sure you would like for me to say that a revival broke out in our church. Then that revival carried over into our city following the funeral. So many people showing up that we turned people away. Granted, many people became aware of making the most of their time. Others definitely used the occasion to share the Gospel.

Honestly, we had some people who never came back to a worship service again after that day.

How do you recover from that?

When some people no longer want to enter the auditorium...
When band members have trouble being on the stage...
When everyone in town is talking about your church but nobody seems to want to attend...

How DO you recover from that?

When Bill died, I saw God showing us a sign of what would come for the church in the next year. I had already been thinking for a while that we were not making the impact we needed to be making. There might be another way to do that.

One year after Bill's passing, we joined together with a church across town. I felt we could be better together and see more lives changed.

Bill's death was not the only reason for making this move. It was not the only factor and not necessarily the greatest one either, but it was the final one. It was a signal of what was ahead.

## - THROWING IN THE TOWEL -

# YOU CAN ONLY STRETCH SO FAR

*by Ron Klabunde*

The number of pastors who throw in the towel is staggering.

Often, this is seen as a negative…a failure…a Kingdom loss. But is it fair to expect that pastors should stay in full-time church ministry for the extent of their working lives, while viewing anything less as defeat?

When pastors throw in the towel, it is often from a place of pain, moral failure, frustration, or exhaustion with wounded souls. This should grieve us.

But is throwing in the towel always a negative…a failure…a Kingdom loss?

Is it possible to throw in the towel - and in doing so - GAIN Kingdom advancement and greater success?

# GIVING UP DOESN'T ALWAYS MEAN YOU ARE WEAK; SOMETIMES IT MEANS YOU ARE STRONG ENOUGH TO LET GO.
## -UNKNOWN-

When my wife (Stefani) and I stepped into church planting, we followed a 13-year dream. This dream was simple. Engage the church in the life of the city by meeting local needs. Engage people in Jesus' mission before they knew it was Jesus' mission. And in doing so, build new discipling relationships with unchurched people, to advance God's Kingdom.

We were not interested in starting another church that was centralized around Sunday mornings. We were not interested in catering to the consumer demands of religious "Christians." We were not interested in growing another large church. We simply wanted to be in relationship with people regardless of their faith background and inspire them to know and live like Jesus.

We pursued this dream by first starting a non-profit. And from that non-profit, we launched a church. This church was forged by the relationships formed through community service. As the church grew, we continued to innovate the non-profit, fine-tuning discipleship with un-churched people in the context of community engagement.

Within a few years, I was leading two organizations – a church and a growing non-profit with over 17,000 volunteers. Today, this non-profit is called Generosity Feeds. With the success of Generosity Feeds, churches around the country began asking us to work with them in their communities.

*I was straddling a picket fence with my feet dangling on both sides.*

Catch the imagery? It hurt.

On one side, I loved the church. I loved the people in the church. These were my friends…my family. I loved how God was changing lives in the church context. I loved teaching and pastoring, and yet, I was drained and bored by the rhythm of Sunday morning services.

On the other side, Generosity Feeds was pulling me into new arenas of ministry…new expressions of discipleship…new and expanding relationships with unchurched people, while providing a broad platform to train and equip churches around America to live Jesus' mission with their city, friends, and family.

A rubber band can only stretch so far…then it snaps.

With two full-time jobs, both focused on advancing God's Kingdom, I was bound to snap. The tension between my love for the people in the church and my passion for discipleship with unchurched people through Generosity Feeds, tore my soul. I could do only one job. If I continued to focus on both, neither would thrive and eventually my family would be hurt. For months, I struggled over what to pursue.

*Sometimes, we must let go of what is good to gain what is great.*

Finally, after sleeping 3 hours one Sunday afternoon – a developing pattern under the mounting stress – Stefani confronted me. "Ron, you can't keep doing what you are doing. You are hurting yourself, and you are not far from hurting our family. You have to choose. Are you going to lead the church or Generosity Feeds?"

The line was drawn.

The next day, I called my coach. With great wisdom, he encouraged me to let the emotions of Sunday taper before making a final decision. Then, through a story, he set me free. For the first time in this part of my journey, I realized it was okay to throw in the towel on good to embrace what was great.

I had fought the good fight. Now I was free to pursue a greater fight.

Today, I am still a pastor, but not in the context of the established church. I pastor my unchurched friends. I pastor our staff. I pastor my children. I mobilize tens-of-thousands of unchurched people into Jesus' mission before they know it is Jesus' mission. I inspire and provide a platform for families, church leaders, business leaders, school administrators, and local communities to live the values of the Kingdom of Heaven here on earth.

I have no regrets. No misgivings. No uncertainty.

Throwing in the towel simply shifted me from good to great as I live out the dream God put in my heart.

## - THROWING IN THE TOWEL -

# I HATE THROWING IN THE TOWEL

*by Scott Hatfield*

*I hate the phrase, "throwing in the towel."* In boxing terms, throwing in the towel communicates a fighter is getting beaten so badly the people in his corner make a conscious decision to stop the fight for the fighter. The referee waves his arms - the fight is over. You're done and your opponent is awarded the victory.

I'll say it again, *I hate the phrase 'throwing in the towel.'* Most of you can identify with me if you're a leader in ministry. If you've been in this game more than a few years, you've learned mental toughness, spiritual grit, and have experienced the difficulty, loneliness, and the pain that ministry brings. You understand it's going to be hard.

Jesus told us this in John 16:33 (NIV) "I have told you these things, so that in Me you may have peace. In this world you will have trouble. But take heart! I have overcome the world." He promised that life will be full of trouble and ministry at times will suck horrifically. Paul tells us in Ephesians 6 we are in a war, so you better put your cup on and fight!

Let me tell you a little about myself. I grew up in a dysfunctional family. My mom had me at the age of 14. My unchurched parents didn't have the tools to change their family legacy. It was a painful 13-years of financial strain, constant fighting, and a multitude of police cars in our driveway. My parents couldn't communicate, wouldn't forgive, and didn't invest in their marriage. As you can imagine, there was plenty of fallout and collateral damage.

I had a radical conversion experience during my junior year of high school. God began to transform my life and called me into full-time ministry during my freshman year of college. I resonate with Isaiah 61:1: (NIV)

> THE SPIRIT OF THE SOVEREIGN LORD IS ON ME, BECAUSE THE LORD HAS ANOINTED ME TO PROCLAIM GOOD NEWS TO THE POOR. HE HAS SENT ME TO BIND UP THE BROKENHEARTED, TO PROCLAIM FREEDOM FOR THE CAPTIVES AND RELEASE FROM DARKNESS FOR THE PRISONERS...
> - ISAIAH 61:1 -

I transferred to bible college, graduated and served in a couple of great churches where I got to sit front row seeing God move in powerful ways for 14 years. Seeing God move, lives changed, and watching the church grow rapidly was normal for me.

During that time, I've had my share of difficult seasons where I've come to know the faithfulness of God. My wife and I went through the pain of unexplained infertility for several years. After much prayer and the help of wonderful doctors, we finally got pregnant.

When our daughter was 20 months old, my wife was diagnosed with breast cancer. There were countless surgeries, the after effects of chemotherapy, and depression. In the middle of that battle, my 27 year old brother was killed. I performed his funeral on our 10 year wedding anniversary. Two months later, my grandfather passed away. Four months after that, my grandmother passed away. I performed each of those funerals. I won't lie, it was a hell of a year.

However, with the ability to look back, we now have a history with Jesus that built upon our faith; creating deep roots and giving us an even greater voice to comfort the hurting and communicate with passion that God is enough!

In the midst of all of this, God put a calling on our family. We would be leaving a great church in Kentucky to lead a church plant outside of Seattle. We would be moving from the buckle of the Bible belt to planting in one of the least churched counties in the US. We went through the assessment process, raised our support, got on the ground, battled spiritual warfare and 13 months later, Resonate Church was born.

It was the best and the worst of ministry. It was the best because we were surrounded with lost people who were hungry for purpose, grace, life and hope. Getting to shape a culture of faith with very little churched baggage was super exciting. One hundred people over five years gave their lives to Christ and went public with their faith through baptism. We experienced incredible life change through God's Spirit moving in people's lives. These are people we still pray for and love very deeply.

It was also the worst of ministry. We were 2,500 miles from everything and everyone that we knew. The "mother church," who was supposed to support us, was not ready to birth us yet. They over promised and under delivered. When we began the process with them, we were to be an intentional church plant. Six months before we launched, we turned into a parachute plant. Most of the churches that planted through our particular organization were parachute plants. Most were small churches with very little support.

Doing ministry at Resonate was extremely challenging. Very few of the people in our church had any history with Jesus before walking through our doors. You can't microwave the discipleship and stewardship process in new believers. Financially it's straining. This issue invoked something I had never battled before - the sin of worry. Then there were the 'religious people.' I thought I might see a unicorn before I ran into 'religious people' in the Pacific Northwest, but nevertheless, dogmatically they would appear.

Staff transitioned out of our church. Some of the people who helped us start the church left after several years - which also is emotionally draining. The pastoral load was often overwhelming in our messy church. Marriages hung in the balance. Addictions were destroying people's lives, not to mention the funerals which were utterly heartbreaking.

I performed a funeral for one family who lost a baby the day after being born. The another funeral for a teenager who passed away unexpectedly. There was the one for the 2 year-old that drowned. And another for a young man who battled mental illness and eventually committed suicide. If you love people, these moments stay with you. They require long-term follow up and spiritual care that is emotionally draining.

We always felt our six years in Washington were uphill. Part of the problem was we didn't do certain things well during that time. For example, I didn't set the right pace for our church. Ministry is not a sprint but a marathon. As leaders, we decide the speed of the race. I ran too fast and climbed too hard. I allowed the church plant to consume most of my time. It invaded my family life and my personal health. It was easy to rationalize it for a multitude of reasons.

The bottom line was: *it was sin.*

Ministry is *never done*. It's not like fighting harder and longer will make all the mess in people's lives go away.

Instead, fight for a sustainable pace. Fight for Sabbath rest. Don't allow ministry to invade the health of your marriage and family. Remember, you are not Jesus (and even he modeled rest). He is the One who builds His church. You are not your title, ministry or church. I struggled with my own drive for the mission of Christ's church. But that drive had a detrimental affect on my health and family. It wasn't God's heart for me and it's not God's heart for you.

In the final year of our church, all our external support was gone. The housing market bubble burst. Twenty percent of the people in our church lost their jobs. This created lots of anxiety for Christ-followers in our church. Even though we had a lot of people now *in Christ*, most of them were still *in debt*. We preached on stewardship, talked transparently about our budget, started offering Financial Peace University, but our new believers were fearful. The weekly giving was very far from our weekly need.

The thought of going back to our external supporters would have been inappropriate after six years in existence. Our small staff was committed to teaching our people about the importance of giving, so we continued to call our people to step up and own the mission of our church.

In the midst of all of this, my wife and I were going through the adoption process. In the middle of the adoption process, my wife got pregnant! Now we were going to have two daughters, six and one half months apart. We were blown away, but our stress levels were high. We received two calls from different churches to come and be a part of their staff in leadership roles. We appreciated the offers yet felt God was clearly saying no.

We believed Seattle was the place God put us to impact lives for Him. Instead of moving on, we challenged our church to step up. We clarified with the church where our hearts were - in Seattle, at Resonate. We retold the story of the church - how it began and who helped get it going. We reminded them of God's calling, and shared with our church about God's incredible provision for it to even be in existence. We told about the generosity of our external supporters who sacrificed to help us get started. I shared these words one day with our church. I said, *"You were the mission and now you are a part of the mission! This is what it means to be a part of the mission. Let's do this."*

It sounded good. It was true. However, the appeal was polarizing - the sacrifice and generosity of some was overwhelming! Others instead chose to hop out of our boat and move on to another church. There is nothing more painful than to see people you've served along side of leave. Especially when they simply choose what's easier instead of digging deep to partner with God and us in these efforts. We couldn't fully understand this, but we started to identify with Jesus after He was betrayed and arrested. Then he watched His closest followers and friends bolt on Him. It was heartbreaking for us, and we weren't being let to our death.

For almost five months, Sarah and I asked God for His will in our lives. We prayed big prayers. We fasted consistently. We took this season to really hear from Jesus. We walked with the wise and relied on the insight of mentors and trusted friends.

Eventually the Holy Spirit was clear. He said to us, "I love you and Sarah. I've called you here. You've been faithful. Now it's time. I'm releasing you. I'm going to take care of you and I'll take care of My Church."

Those words were bittersweet for us. Sarah and I have always been called to go somewhere and then been released from our current position. This time God was releasing us without a clear place to go. I'll be honest, I like the first way better.

The story of how God called Abraham to go, without telling him where 'Go,' would lead him has always intrigued me. Of course, not intriguing enough to desire it myself. The God we serve is the God of both calling and releasing, regardless of the order. God had ushered in His peace within us about this decision.

The day we communicated this with our church? Now that was incredibly hard. We were blown away. Almost every person was so amazing (there were a few who were not). But their words, appreciation and gratitude were overwhelming!

We left Seattle and moved back to Kentucky to be closer to our family. This allowed us to get our feet under us again and to heal from ministry as we anticipated the birth of our third daughter. I tried at first to hustle to figure out what was next for us in ministry. Then I came to the realization that God would take care of everything. We moved back home and I started working for a construction company. This job was sort of ironic. Me working for a construction company? My tools are some of the cleanest on the planet.

After six months with that company, I took an interim position with a church I worked with prior to our time in Seattle. In this setting, I was able to step back into ministry and help them out while listening to see what God had for us in the future. It was a great season for our family to breathe, rest and have our tanks filled back up.

## LESSONS FROM THE TOWEL:

Solomon tells us that there are seasons for everything. These seasons can be long or short. Thankfully, God in His Sovereignty, determines the length for us. I've always gravitated towards Paul's words in Ephesians 4:1:

AS A PRISONER FOR THE LORD, THEN,
I URGE YOU TO LIVE A LIFE WORTHY OF THE CALLING
YOU HAVE RECEIVED.
- EPHESIANS 4:1 -

Wherever you are, live out the calling that God's given you! Love people, serve well, lead with courage, and cast a big vision of what it means to live for Christ. Make your life count! Some of my ministry friends have pastored in the same church their entire ministry career. For others, their time in ministry looks like they were contestants on The Amazing Race. The key is to live in the seasons that God gives you. Be in tune with the Holy Spirit so you live out the calling God has placed in your heart. Do not compare your calling to others. In the end, you will not give an account of someone else's calling—only your own. Our role is to live worthy lives of the calling we received!

## GOD'S GOT YOU:

Take a moment and look back at your own personal history with God. Think about the endless sermons you've preached. The wisdom you've imparted to others about the faithfulness and care of your Heavenly Father. He's the Good Shepherd in Psalm 23. He's the God who parted the Red Sea in the midst of extreme circumstances to deliver His people. Jesus is the one who takes a kid's lunchable and feeds thousands of people. He's the one who died on a cross to conquer sin and resurrected to defeat the grave. He is faithful. He loves you with a relentless love. He has not forgotten you in the midst of your painful season!

Mike and Debbie Breaux have been mentors to Sarah and me for a long time. In the midst of the hard season, the Holy Spirit spoke through them when they said, "God is for you." Those words were words that we needed to hear. Maybe you need to hear these words.

God is for you!

He knows your name. He knows your situation. His heart breaks over your broken heart. He knows what's next for you. God's got ya!

## YOU ARE MORE TIRED & HURT THAN YOU REALIZE:

You are more tired and hurt than you realize. A close circle of friends shared this wisdom with me. At the time, I wasn't sure I even knew what they were talking about until that miserable season was over.

Even the best seasons of ministry are filled with faith-filled risks. There are emotional withdrawals. You will find yourself spiritually dry. And of course, the enemy will bring extreme warfare in these seasons. If you're in the middle or on the backside of a difficult season—take the time to process this with the Lord and the Lord's people. It's human nature to just jump to the next thing and move on. Do yourself a favor - resist that temptation! Don't' do it!

God wants to be your Father. Let Him love you and care for you. The Holy Spirit will reveal what you need to know and what you need to hear. Let Him heal you and prepare you for what's next.

Then make sure you talk this out well with your spouse and family. They need you to process well. They will need your help processing their experiences. Talk this out with mentors, Godly friends, other pastors and even a christian counselor. We had them all on our team and it made all the difference. I would also recommend grabbing the book, The Land Between, by Jeff Manion. It's a powerful book about transition through hard times.


## SUCCESS = FAITHFULNESS!

Understand God's heart for success. We think success is always tied to growth, numbers and bigger ministries and churches. Growth is important but it's doesn't necessarily mean success. God never promises us worldly success. He actually promises us the opposite. In John chapter 6, Jesus fed thousands of people, taught a huge crowds, and performed miracles. What happened next?

Most of the people left.

If it happened to Jesus—it will happen to you. God calls us to faithfulness. Whether you're a youth pastor in a small church, an associate in a medium sized church, a missionary in a foreign land with no followers and no converts—God's calling for us is faithfulness. We're called to live for Christ and to be faithful to Him. Obedience and faithfulness are incredibly important to God. He tells us that if we love Him, we'll obey Him. Jesus also tells us in Matthew 25 that when we stand before the Father these are the words that we want to hear, *"Well done, good and faithful servant!"*

Whether you need to throw in the towel, or pick it up and keep chasing God's heart to see what He has next - remember, He is faithful. He's for you and He's calling you to faithfulness!

## - THROWING IN THE TOWEL -

# THE RHYTHM OF RELEASE

*by Dave Milam*

Hidden behind an auto body shop and beside a metal fabrication mill, sat our office. The church was still portable, so this gave us a cozy place to work when the Starbucks was packed. Our bookkeeper didn't have an office there. Peggy lived in Atlanta. She was fantastic at balancing our account and even better at breaking bad news.

I had received this call only two other times in the nine years our church had been alive.

"Funds are low and we can't make payroll," she said. Short and sweet. Like ripping off a band-aid fast. It's the most humane way to do it.

I hung up the phone. The dusty books on the shelf had probably seen trouble like this before. Nobody ever read them. They were donated and gave our church office a cozy vibe. Next to the leather bound American Standard Bible sat a Veggie Tales VHS. Bob the Tomato looked so carefree. I stood dazed, envious of his happy-go-lucky grin. I wished I was a tomato.

I had taken hundreds of leadership hits in the past, but this blow felt different. I wasn't okay this time. It was February, the strongest giving month of the year, and our church was nearly nine years old.

My wife, Anne, took the news much better than I did. She got a job and we began saving money and praying for clarity. Hope was waning and I sensed it was time to wrap up this season of leadership.

Sometimes God concludes seasons of ministry quickly and almost overnight calls a leader to the next critical assignment. Other times, it is a long slow burn. This moment became the first downbeat in God's rhythm of release on my call to pastor the church my family had sacrificed to plant.

As March ended, the church's account continued to be dangerously low. We moved the donated books to storage and closed down the church's office space, hoping to lighten our financial load as we entered summer. I knew cuts wouldn't be enough to sustain us. Our church typically hemorrhages financially each summer. It's our rainy-day season. My spit-ball math told me by sometime mid-June I would be talking payroll with Peggy again.

My wife and I continued praying for clarity, and after re-running my financial forecasts, agreed it was time to tell the elders about what God had been stirring in our hearts.

Our elders meet in the the strangest places. Often we'll meet in a hotel lobby. We always skip the complimentary happy hour, though there are some meetings we could really use that kind of support. That night, we met on the geriatric side of the Chick Fil A (near the restrooms). The seniors played bingo there on Tuesday mornings.

After rolling through the standard business of the day, I dropped the bomb. "Guys, I think it's time to create a transition plan for my position. I am done. I have fulfilled everything to which God has called me and I have nothing left to give."

The temperature of the room immediately changed. Even the coffee and waffle fries grew cold.

I continued, "I'm not leaving tomorrow, but I sense God is releasing me from leadership at One Life Church, and I want to transition well. So, let's figure this out together."

I lead with great men, so their response was gracious and spirit filled. And that night sounded like another steady beat in God's *rhythm of release*.

Over the next three months, I worked hard and closed my eyes tight. Like you do when someone throws a rock at your face. I think it's your body's way of softening the blow. Knowing at any moment money would run out and I'd be on the street, I buttoned up my resume. I began putting my name 'out there,' confident God was moving ahead of me.

My efforts to get a job were met with silence.

It was August when I first began to peek through my scrunched eyes to survey the wreckage. I had braced for impact all summer long. Yet my darkest fears were never realized. Our community was still standing and each month brought new people and a steady paycheck. God had been unexpectedly faithful and met our financial needs that season. Survival was no less than a miracle. In fact, God increased the church's financial position by 200%.

That's when the phone rang.

A church in our area had recently outgrown her building and relocated several miles down the road. I had inquired about their property at the time of their move, but that road appeared to be a dead end.

"Pastor Dave, our team met and is interested in leasing our old building to your church...if you are interested." the caller said.

I told them we were interested, scribbled down some details on a napkin then hung up the phone.

A strange combination of excitement, anger and confusion flooded me. I remember praying, "God, what are you doing? You were crystal clear when You untethered me from leadership just a few months ago. And I have heard Your steady *rhythm of release* and now You give us a freak'n building? I'm earnestly trying to follow, but I have no idea what You're doing."

I was so confused. No one seemed to know what God was up to. Least of all, me.

Everybody had an opinion. One of our church's elders told me, "We believe God was just waiting for you to completely surrender before He was going to bless our church."

I'll be honest, that would preach.

Yet when I asked my friends and mentors outside the church, they would say, "Seems like God is getting your church ready for the next guy."

I believe both were true.

God's *rhythm of release* continued, but this time it wasn't the clear sound of a kick drum pounding change on the floor of my heart. Instead, it was a rest. The silence between notes that makes you lean in a little. The pause that makes a rhythm unique and memorable.

Over the next few months, our church experienced an enormous blessing by one of the most generous churches I've ever known. Veggie Tales came out of storage and we held opening services in our new facility in December 2014. The vibe of our community was electric. Finances were strong, and people were renewed with excitement.

I did my best to bury my feeling of release deep in those places where you bury all the scary stuff you never want to see again. And I vowed to lead strong. The problem with burying something God told you is, it doesn't stay buried for long. Within months of moving into our new facility, I heard the whisper reengage, "It's time."

One of my leadership mentors is a Jedi Master named Carl. He talks in riddles, like Yoda, but is much taller. Carl is the closest thing to a prophet I've ever met. It's as if his mind is virtually connected to God's and his timing is always impeccable.

When Carl offered to drive a couple hours out of his way to come see me, I knew something was up. I'm not that important and this guy is in high demand. He arrived at our church and ogled the facility before we settled in for a Panera lunch at carb central.

"I want to tell you three stories," he told me.

I countered with silence and a nod.

"We did a study several years ago and discovered that in the lifecycle of an organization, there are four different kinds of leaders. Some leaders are designed to start the organization, others are wired to grow it, still some leaders are passionate about maintaining the organization, then finally someone is called to kill it. It's rare the same person does all four tasks." He paused and sipped his water.

He continued, "I also did some research on leaders in their mid 40's. By the way, how old are you?" he asked.

"I'm 44," I replied.

"Hmmmm, interesting. We discovered those leaders increase their effectiveness when they move from doing what they 'can do' to what they 'should do.'"

My mind began to blank and I remembered Bob the Tomato sitting on the shelf. His nauseating smile now stretched across my face. God had sent a prophet to confirm my release. The clarity was undeniable.

In an instant, I felt my stomach untie itself and peace swallow me whole. It was as if Jesus calmed my inner storm with just a few words over a bread bowl and chips.

When I regained consciousness, Carl had just wrapped up his third story.

He dabbed the corner of his mouth with a napkin and asked, "So Dave, what are you hearing me say?"

I knew the question was a trap, set by the most skillful of hunters. And I wanted nothing left to question this time. I was already confident that God had spoken, but I wanted to be absolutely sure. So, I fleeced again.

"No, no, no, no, no. Not this time, Carl," I responded. "I'm not playing this Jedi mind game with you today. This time, I want you to tell me exactly what you're trying to say. No guesswork here."

I knew getting him to speak directly would be an epic fight, but I was prepared for the skirmish. Like a training scene from Star Wars, master and apprentice battled it out. Each warrior fighting for the right to hear truth spoken.

We dueled. And finally, he surrendered.

"Dave, it's time," he whispered

Those three words became the final beat in a slow and steady two year *rhythm of release*. I smiled and sipped my water. "I know." I said.

"I know."

Over the years, I've discovered that the healthiest leadership transitions happen in the context of a slow and steady *rhythm of release*. Thankfully, God cares enough to gently loosen our grip before asking us to let go. It's that long slow burn that grants margin to hand off the baton well and care about those we've served over the years.

The most effective leaders have become experts at thriving in the midst of struggle and have often used roadblocks to catalyze personal and organizational growth. They've learned to allow the hard knocks of leading forge the kind of character that only shows up after you weathered a few storms. And they know when to quit.

Hearing release requires that you stay in the fight. One lonely beat cannot create a rhythm by itself. Rhythm requires multiple beats and rests looping together over time. It's not until you've taken a few hits and rested; then taken a several more that you will ever hear the *rhythm of release.*

# TEN COUNT
# CONTRIBUTORS
## AND STORYTELLERS

# CONTRIBUTORS

## Aaron M. Brockett, Lead Pastor
## Traders Point Christian Church - Indianapolis, IN

Aaron Brockett serves as the lead pastor of Traders Point Christian Church, a growing multi-campus congregation with a 180-year history of serving the far northwest side of Indianapolis. Since 2007, God has used Aaron's passion for multiplying and developing leaders to inspire and grow the church's congregation to over 6000 weekly attenders at two campuses with a third location opening in 2016. Traders Point not only makes a global impact, the congregation has a unique platform to share the Gospel with Indianapolis and mobilize a movement that influences people in the city for Christ. Aaron and Lindsay, his wife of 17 years, are blessed with four great children--Conor, Campbell, Kennedi, and Kadence.

## Nate Bush, Lead Pastor
## New City Church - Albuquerque, NM

I believe there is no greater cause on earth than the mission of God at work through the family of God. I serve as the Lead Pastor of New City Church in Albuquerque, NM. Prior to planting New City Church in 2010 I spent 13 years in youth ministry. I married my high school sweet heart Vanessa and together we have 2 boys, Micah and Corban, and a girl named Evangeline.

## Trevor DeVage, Lead Pastor
## Christ's Church Mason - Mason, OH

My day job is preaching/teaching the mysteries of God to the known world, but primarily I do so with my good friends at Christ's Church in Mason, Ohio. I love family, honesty, the ability to laugh and make others laugh, music, art, photography and anything else remotely creative. People intrigue me. Silence scares me. God amazes me and frustrates me. I am a disciple long before I will ever be a leader. Sometimes I exaggerate, but not on purpose, more for the sake of a good story to make someone laugh. As my wife says I don't know a lot about one thing, but know a little about a lot and so I can conversate with most people about most things. The Word of God inspires me and perplexes me. I wish God would speak out loud to me because I am not good at finding things that are hidden. There are many other things that make up the DNA that is me, but that is just a start.

## Marques "Big Cleve" Evans, Lead Pastor
## Revolution 216 - Cleveland, OH

Pastor Marques "Big Cleve" Evans is married to his beautiful wife, Krista, and they have four children: Darnell, Nadia, Micah and Malaya. He started the Revolution 216 as Lead Pastor in October 2011. Pastor Marques was saved as a young adult after a spiritual encounter with The Most High on an airplane coming from college. Although he grew up in church, he didn't really have a relationship with The Messiah.

## Scott Hatfield, Lead Pastor
## Gateway Church - Kansas City, MO

Scott is the Lead Pastor of Gateway Church in Kansas City, MO and graduate of Cincinnati Christian University. Scott loves his wife Sarah and partners with her to raise three dangerous women for God's purposes. Help people find and follow Jesus. Lead boldly and challenge the church to be a dangerous movement for God's glory and His Kingdom.

## Ron Klabunde, Founder and CEO
## Generosity Feeds - Sterling, VA

Ron is the Founder and CEO of Generosity Feeds – a national non-profit that mobilizes thousands of volunteers in cities around America to address the needs of hungry children in their area through meal packaging events. As speaker, trainer, and coach, Ron advocates generosity while equipping organizations and leaders to engage in a mission that helps bring peace and prosperity to their cities. He specializes in assisting businesses, non-profits, and churches in community engagement and targeted needs assessments.

## Jerel Law,
## Pastor, Communicator & Author - Huntersville, NC

Jerel is a gifted communicator and pastor with over twenty years of full-time ministry experience. He holds his undergraduate degree from the University of North Carolina at Chapel Hill and an MDiv from Gordon-Conwell Theological Seminary. Jerel has served churches in the roles of church planter, lead pastor, discipleship pastor, and teaching pastor. Currently he is a church planter with Radiant Life Fellowship in Huntersville, NC. He has written four books in a tween action/adventure fiction series published by Thomas Nelson. He thinks that stuff is great, but he's most excited about his relationship with Jesus and his three amazing kids.

## JON McCLARON, CAMPUS PASTOR & TEACHING TEAM
## LIFEPOINT CHURCH - RALEIGH, NC

Jon loves his wife Kris and enjoys spending time with their three children Jordan, Jessica and Desiree. He also enjoys playing a round of golf and has a deep love of college basketball. He's been fortunate to have plenty of both while living in Raleigh, NC for the past 17 years. Feels most like himself - talking about following Jesus over a cup of coffee; teaching; and loves to see people's lives changed by the transforming grace of Jesus.

## DAVE MILAM, LEAD PASTOR
## ONE LIFE CHURCH - CONCORD, NC

Dave Milam is a gifted leader & communicator whose right brained style of delivery helps his listener connect and remember God's truth in a uniquely visual way. God has called him to inspire christians to become stronger leaders and more influential disciples in their workplace, school and community. Dave is pastor, visionary and founder of One Life Church in Charlotte, North Carolina. Dave, his wife Anne, and their four children currently live in Charlotte, North Carolina.

## AARON MONTS, CHURCH PLANTER & FOUNDER
## SEATTLE PARTNERSHIP - SEATTLE, WA

Aaron Monts was the founding pastor of IKON Christian Community in San Francisco which was featured in the NY Times, Huffington Post, and Bay Citizen. He was also featured as an important voice for spirituality in the "Power Issue" of San Francisco Magazine. In 2015 he began working towards starting a new church in Seattle. Beyond starting a new church, Aaron is currently working on a dissertation for his PhD at Johnson University. In his writing, speaking, and living, Aaron is committed to expressing a Christian faith that is beautifully complex, unimaginably just, and excruciatingly gracious.

## DERRICK PUCKETT, LEAD PASTOR & CHURCH PLANTER
## RENEWAL CHURCH - CHICAGO, IL

Derrick Puckett is the Lead Pastor and Church Planter of Renewal Church of Chicago in Chicago, IL. He and his wife, Kaley, moved to Chicago in 2013 to plant a Gospel centered disciple making multi-ethnic church. Derrick has a bachelor's degree from Indiana University and a Masters of Divinity from Mid America Baptist Theological Seminary. Derrick and Kaley have 3 beautiful daughters: Ramiyah, Elyana, Isabelle and a soon to be fourth.

## JASON REHMEL, LEAD PASTOR
## EASTSIDE CHRISTIAN CHURCH - CINCINNATI, OH

Jason Rehmel is the Lead Pastor of Eastside Christian Church on the east side of Cincinnati, Ohio. He and his wife Tera have two children and two dogs and zero cats. He is originally from southern Indiana and is a lifelong Indiana University basketball fan - which has been a painful endeavor some years. He writes about his experiences as a pastor on his blog: unlikleypastor.com.

## DANNY SCHAFFNER, JR., SENIOR PASTOR
## FIRST CHRISTIAN CHURCH - CHAMPAIGN IL

Danny Schaffner, Jr. loves Jesus, his wife, family, and the local church. He has been blessed to be married to his wife for over 20 years. They have 4 boys, 1 daughter in law, and two grandkids. He has served as a youth pastor, teaching pastor, church planter, and Senior Pastor. In 2007 he planted a multi-ethnic, urban church work in Tampa, FL. He currently serves as Senior Pastor at First Christian Church in Champaign, IL.

## CHAD SIMPKINS, LEAD PASTOR
## VARSITY CHURCH - CHAPEL HILL, NC

Chad and his wife Kara lead Varsity Church in Chapel Hill, North Carolina, a church they planted in 2011. He has held the roles of Youth Pastor and Campus Pastor at churches in New Jersey and Virginia. His heart bleeds for people far from God. He also loves working with church planters and their spouses. He and his wife have 3 kids and a 17-year old Jack Russell named Myrtle.

## CHRIS STOVALL,
## TEAM MEMBER AND CONSULTANT FOR GENERIS

Chris is a proven leader and entrepreneur with a servant's heart. He has served in full-time ministry leadership and as a pastor for 25 years while also starting and growing several companies. Chris has a driving passion for the local church and to lay himself open to do whatever he can to see the local church prosper and grow.

Chris is a member of the Generis team working as a consultant to churches in the area of generosity. Whether it is leading a church through generosity initiatives/campaigns, coaching them in developing best practices in the area of generosity to enhance their culture of generosity and/or conduct a Generosity Audit to assess a church's culture of generosity while recommending future action steps. The Generis mission is to accelerate generosity toward God-inspired vision.

## DEREK SWEATMAN, LEAD PASTOR
## ATLANTA CHRISTIAN CHURCH - ATLANTA, GA

Derek is pastor of Atlanta Christian Church, a downtown congregation located one block north of Centennial Olympic Park on historic Marietta Street. A native of Atlanta, Derek has a vested interest in his home city, and a penchant for the local church living on the front side of spiritual healing and social repair inside southern communities. On the side he collects records, runs, follows the Tedeschi Trucks Band around, and is adjunct professor of Biblical Studies at Point University. His favorite Grateful Dead show is March 8, 1977, Cornell University. "The best version of 'Jack Straw' is in that show."

## JONATHAN WILLIAMS, LEAD PASTOR
## FOREFRONT CHURCH - NEW YORK, NY

Jonathan Williams is a writer, speaker, and pastor. Jonathan currently serves as the Senior Pastor of Forefront Church in New York, NY, a progressive Church that works to bring a just and generous Christianity to New York City.

Jonathan has spoken at several national conferences including Exponential, Eastern Christian Conference, and the Organization of Progressive Evangelicals Network. Jonathan's writing appears in the Huffington Post, Christian Standard, and Rebel Storytellers publications.

Jonathan was named one of the top 40 leaders under 40 by Christian Standard Magazine. He currently resides in Brooklyn, NY with his spouse and two daughters.

Made in the USA
Charleston, SC
29 April 2016